# Your Child's First Pet:

## A Parent's Guide to Ensuring Success

By Amy Brayfield

*With Foreword By Debbie McKnight, M.S., C.P.D.T.*

# YOUR CHILD'S FIRST PET: A PARENT'S GUIDE TO ENSURING SUCCESS

Copyright © 2011 Atlantic Publishing Group, Inc.
1405 SW 6th Avenue • Ocala, Florida 34471 • Phone 800-814-1132 • Fax 352-622-1875
Web site: www.atlantic-pub.com • E-mail: sales@atlantic-pub.com
SAN Number: 268-1250

Library of Congress Cataloging-in-Publication Data

Brayfield, Amy.
   Your child's first pet : a parent's guide to ensuring success / by Amy Brayfield.
      p. cm.
   Includes bibliographical references and index.
   ISBN-13: 978-1-60138-394-5 (alk. paper)
   ISBN-10: 1-60138-394-0 (alk. paper)
   1. Pets. I. Title.
   SF411.5.B725 2010
   636.088'7--dc22

                              2010007591

PROJECT MANAGER: Erin Everhart • PEER REVIEWER: Marilee Griffin
ASSISTANT EDITOR: Holly Marie Gibbs • INTERIOR DESIGN: Samantha Martin
FRONT COVER DESIGN: Jackie Miller • millerjackiej@gmail.com

Printed on Recycled Paper

Printed in the United States

We recently lost our beloved pet "Bear," who was not only our best and dearest friend but also the "Vice President of Sunshine" here at Atlantic Publishing. He did not receive a salary but worked tirelessly 24 hours a day to please his parents. Bear was a rescue dog that turned around and showered myself, my wife, Sherri, his grandparents Jean, Bob, and Nancy, and every person and animal he met (maybe not rabbits) with friendship and love. He made a lot of people smile every day.

We wanted you to know that a portion of the profits of this book will be donated to The Humane Society of the United States.  *–Douglas & Sherri Brown*

---

The human-animal bond is as old as human history. We cherish our animal companions for their unconditional affection and acceptance. We feel a thrill when we glimpse wild creatures in their natural habitat or in our own backyard.

Unfortunately, the human-animal bond has at times been weakened. Humans have exploited some animal species to the point of extinction.

The Humane Society of the United States makes a difference in the lives of animals here at home and worldwide. The HSUS is dedicated to creating a world where our relationship with animals is guided by compassion. We seek a truly humane society in which animals are respected for their intrinsic value, and where the human-animal bond is strong.

Want to help animals? We have plenty of suggestions. Adopt a pet from a local shelter, join The Humane Society and be a part of our work to help companion animals and wildlife. You will be funding our educational, legislative, investigative and outreach projects in the U.S. and across the globe.

Or perhaps you'd like to make a memorial donation in honor of a pet, friend or relative? You can through our Kindred Spirits program. And if you'd like to contribute in a more structured way, our Planned Giving Office has suggestions about estate planning, annuities, and even gifts of stock that avoid capital gains taxes.

Maybe you have land that you would like to preserve as a lasting habitat for wildlife. Our Wildlife Land Trust can help you. Perhaps the land you want to share is a backyard— that's enough. Our Urban Wildlife Sanctuary Program will show you how to create a habitat for your wild neighbors.

So you see, it's easy to help animals. And The HSUS is here to help.

2100 L Street NW • Washington, DC 20037 • 202-452-1100
www.hsus.org

# Dedication

*For Jason, Olwen, and Thor —*
*and of course, Little Foot.*

## Acknowledgements:

I owe several people thanks for their help in making this book happen.

Erin Everhart, my editor at Atlantic Publishing, walked me through the publishing process with tremendous talent and generosity — and an eye for adding serial commas.

Thanks to Jennifer, Andy, Mallory, and Allissa Peterson; Linda and Jeremy Richland; Maggie and Lily Hutchinson; Greg, Alison, Emily, and Charles Harris; Julie, Ron, and Lena Garfield; Karen and Daniel Whiting; Andrea, Benjamin, and Cleo Clifford; Jonathan Reed, D.V.M.; Sarah and Kimberly Reid; Kristin, Michael, Haley, and David Warren; Holly, Jake, and Caroline Arnold; and Louise, Derek, Sasha, and Meredith Callaghan — they were all kind enough to share their stories and answer my many questions.

Thanks, too, to Kelly Gavin, D.V.M, Cindy Ragoni, D.V.M, and Eric Robertson, D.V.M, who helped me to keep my facts straight. Appreciation also goes to Julia Windisch, Abigail Bergman, Laura Klein, Jerry Donaldson, and Emily Berger for helping me to better understand the different ways animals find families. I am also grateful to my lovely mothers-in-law, Barbara and Donna, and my father-in-law, Abe, for all the free baby-sitting while I wrote, and to my family, Jason, Olwen, and Thor for feeding the cat when I was too busy.

# Table of Contents

## Chapter 8: You Decided on Your Pet — Now What?      191

## Chapter 9: Pet Care 101      219

## Chapter 10: Challenges      243

## Chapter 11: Living With Your New Pet 261

## Conclusion: ... And They Lived Happily Ever After 273

## Internet References 275

## Bibliography 279

## Biography 283

## Index 285

# Foreword

A Parent's Guide to
Ensuring Success

L assie, Benji, Old Yeller. They make kids and dogs look like they go together naturally — like peas and carrots. However, those dogs are trained professionals, and a pet the whole family can love does not usually happen without some hard work. If you are wondering what pet would be the best choice for your family, you have come to the right place.

As a dog trainer, I have many people asking for recommendations on what type of dog to get for their children. They generally want something easy going, sturdy, non-shedding, not too big, and well trained from day one. Since these "fairy tale" dogs are few and far between in the real world, parents need some guidance in choosing a new dog — or any new pet — and what to expect. In *Your Child's First Pet: A Parent's Guide to Ensuring Success*, Amy Brayfield does a great job of laying out exactly what to expect when getting a new pet for your child. People may be surprised by just how much time, money, and effort is required in caring for an animal. For those folks, Brayfield gives easy, less time-consuming options for parents to consider.

Any new pet is going to take time and commitment. Generally speaking, the pets that are the most engaging and involved in your family are the ones that take the most work. A dog is commonly called "man's best friend," but like any good friendship, time and effort are required. In exchange for that time and effort though, you get the best friend anyone could wish for. A fish will be lower maintenance, but also less enjoyment if your child is hoping for a pet he or she can play with and touch. A cat or bird will interact with your child in a different way than a puppy wagging its tail when you come home. Knowing your child and your own commitment level will ensure you both get the most enjoyment from your new pet.

Whatever pet you select will ultimately be your responsibility. In my training class, parents often bring their child because "it is his/her dog." I welcome children in my classes and agree that they need to be involved in the care and training of "their" dog. However, if the parent is not 100 percent on board with getting and caring for the pet, then it is unfair to that animal to bring it into the household. Take Brayfield's advice and make sure the whole family is ready before bringing a new pet home!

— Debbie McKnight

## About Debbie McKnight

Debbie McKnight, M.S., C.P.D.T. is a professional pet dog trainer with more than eight years of experience. She was one of the first Certified Pet Dog Trainers in Texas and has her master's degree in behavior analysis. She is a strong advocate of clicker training and positive reinforcement. McKnight teaches group classes and private lessons specializing in manners for family pet dogs. She shares her home and her heart with a 9-year-old German Shepherd, Kyra.

# Introduction

The Family Pet

*Is your family ready for a new addition?*

Perhaps your daughter has been wistfully eyeing the neighbor's fluffy white cat, or your son has begun begging for his own hamster. Maybe you have been nostalgically remembering your own childhood dog and want your children to have the same great experiences that you had; or maybe you never had a pet as a child, and want your children to grow up with an animal friend. Whatever your motivation, you have started to wonder whether it is time to expand your family to include a new pet.

Pets are an integral part of childhood for many people; about 90 percent of children live in a home with an animal at some point during their childhoods, according to research by Gail F. Melson, professor emeritus of developmental studies at Purdue University in Indiana and author of *Why the Wild Things Are: Animals in the Lives of Children.* Images of families with pets surround us: the all-American Tanners on the sitcom "Full House" played in the backyard with their golden retriever, Comet, while the cartoon Simpsons have Santa's Little Helper, a dog as boisterous as the rest of the family; even the Munsters had Igor the bat. One of President Barack Obama's first acts in office was to let his daughters choose their first family pet: a Portuguese water dog named Bo. Families and pets seem to belong together.

In fact, pets can benefit families in numerous ways. Though becoming a pet owner entails certain responsibilities, it also comes with certain benefits that can make your family healthier and happier.

## Pets Can Help Your Child Learn

Playing with your pet is fun, and studies show that interacting with pets also improves a child's ability to reason and think complex thoughts. Toddlers who have pets demonstrate more advanced cognitive development and better motor skills than toddlers who grow up in pet-free homes, according to a 1989 study conducted by Laurel A. Redefer and Joan F. Goodman. In-depth studies into the exact benefits pets can have on children are rare — 1989 was the most recent year that concluded such evidence — but the Eunice Kennedy Shriver National Institute of Child Health and Human Development, which is part of the National Institutes of Health, reported in October 2009 it is breaking new ground on more conclusive studies that show a pet's tangible benefit to children.

Pets can offer a nonthreatening place for children to practice skills, especially reading and physical development. Children are incredibly comfortable reading in front of their pets, according to researcher Mary Renck Jalongo, Ph.D., an education professor at Indiana University of Pennsylvania and author of the book *The World of Children and Their Companion Animals*. In the study, Jalongo asked children to read aloud in front of a peer, an adult, and a dog and measured their stress levels in front of each. The children's stress levels were significantly lower when they read in front of the dog than when they read in front of an adult or peer.

These facts do not mean that adopting a cat will transform your child into a pint-sized Einstein, but a pet can have a lifelong impact on your child's learning abilities.

## Pets Can Help Your Child Cope with Challenges

Growing up can be full of challenges, and pets provide plenty of unconditional love and support to help children get through the tough times.

Seventy percent of children say that they confide in their pets when they are worried, scared, or have secrets because they feel like their pets are trustworthy and love them no matter what, according to a study by Alan Beck, Ph.D., at the Purdue University Center for the Animal-Human Bond. Another study, conducted at the University of Michigan in 1985, showed that 75 percent of children between ages 10 and 14 turned to their pets for comfort when they felt upset. When parents rated their children's anxiety and withdrawal, kids who turned to pets for comfort fared better than children who did not draw on their pets for support or did not have pets.

Pets can also help children who are struggling to fit in socially. In one of Melson's studies, children were asked to offer advice to other children who were having trouble making friends. The most frequently suggested answer: Get a pet. Not only did kids say a pet provided friendship and companionship, they also suggested that it gives children something to talk about and a point of connection with other kids.

When times get tough — because of social or learning challenges, switching schools, or more serious problems such as death in the family, parents' divorce, or serious illness — a pet can help children cope better with the difficulties in front of them.

## Pets Help Your Child Develop Nurturing Skills

A century ago, older children helped their parents care for their younger siblings; but today's working parents, preschool agencies, and smaller families, as well as more-organized child care with nannies and after-school programs, give children fewer firsthand opportunities to learn nurturing skills. Having a pet can help children learn how to care for others. Being responsible for things like feeding, grooming, and caring for a pet helps children develop responsibility and empathy.

Children are more likely to have the opportunity to learn nurturing skills with pets than with younger siblings. One of Melson's studies found that children older than 3 who had pets spent about 10.3 minutes each day engaged in caretaking activities for their pets — while children who had younger siblings spent an average of just 2.4 minutes each day caring for their brothers and sisters.

Nurturing skills play an important part in social and emotional development by helping children develop compassion, communication, curiosity, and cooperation. Pets are a gender-neutral way to introduce your child to the importance of caring for another living being: Unlike other nurturing activities, such as baby-sitting, which are considered "girl" activities, pet care is not perceived along gender lines.

## Pets Can Make Your Children Healthier

Growing up with pets may help make your children resistant to allergies, asthma, and other common childhood health issues.

Children who were exposed to two or more dogs or cats as babies are half as likely to suffer from common indoor and outdoor allergies — including pet dander, dust mites, ragweed, or grass — than children who grew up in pet-free homes, according to research conducted at the Medical College of Georgia. In the study headed by Dennis Ownby, M.D., pediatrician and head of the college's department of allergy and immunology, researchers tracked a group of children from birth to about age 7 to determine whether having a pet impacted their experience with allergies. Other studies have shown a similar decrease in asthma for children who live in homes with pets.

The benefits are not just for kids, either. Cat owners are nearly 30 percent less likely to suffer a heart attack, with the same outcome likely for dog owners, according to a 2008 study by the University of Minnesota's Stroke Institute in Minneapolis. Researchers at the University of California Los Angeles (UCLA) Center and

School of Nursing also found that dogs helped people with heart failure by improving heart and lung functions.

## Pets Can Strengthen Your Family Bond

A pet brings together your family by giving you a set of activities to share. A pet needs grooming, feeding, and play time; working together on these activities gives your family regular, shared goals.

A pet can bring big benefits to your child and to your family, so choosing the right one is important. This book will help you decide whether your family is ready for a pet and help you sort through the options to choose the pet that is best for you, based on your child's age and personality and your family's lifestyle. It will give you information on some of the most popular pets, including dogs, cats, birds, fish, and more exotic animals, so that you have a clear idea of the responsibilities and costs associated with each type of pet. Finally, this book will help you prepare for that happy day when your family brings home its first pet, answer some of the questions new pet owners frequently face, and help you become healthy, happy pet owners.

Choosing a pet can be a wonderful way to grow your family. This book will give you the tools you need to choose wisely and have a lifetime of happy pet ownership.

# Chapter 1

Is Your Family Ready for a Pet?

What is it about a pet that makes it seem like the perfect finishing touch to a perfect family? There are many reasons to welcome a pet into your family, and the fun, companionship, and entertainment of pet ownership are all good ones. But it is important to remember that playing in the park together is only one part of becoming a pet owner. Pets are living things that require a great deal of care. They need feeding, grooming, and regular veterinary care. They need exercise and love, even when it is rainy or cold outside or when you are exhausted. They are a full-time commitment.

You may be excited about the idea of bringing home a pet, but this chapter is designed to help you decide if your family is really ready to take on the job of pet ownership. By considering your family's lifestyle, expectations, location, previous experience with pets, and long-term plans — in addition to the costs and maintenance of pets — you can determine whether your family is ready for a pet or if it would be wise to wait a little longer before you invite a new member to join the family. If you bring home a pet to join your family before you are ready to be pet owners, you may end up with wasted money, heartbroken children, and a pet that needs to find a new home.

## Lifestyle

Your lifestyle is a key factor when it comes to determining whether your family is ready to have a pet. If your lifestyle does not lend itself to responsible pet ownership, then you may have to be willing to make accommodations to your lifestyle if you have your heart set on bringing home a pet. Here are some questions to ask as you consider getting a pet:

### How often are you home?

If you work all day while your kids are at school and spend most of your weekends out of the house, think carefully about the type of pet that will best fit your busy schedule. Lower-maintenance pets, such as fish or reptiles, are typically fine when alone for long stretches of time and actually prefer solitude. Most pets need attention and love — not just food and water — so if your pet will be spending most of its time alone in an empty house or in the backyard, it might be wiser to wait until your schedule has more free time. On the other hand, if your family spends plenty of weekends at home or you work from a home office, a pet such as a dog or cat might be a great addition to your lifestyle, giving you a daytime break and a friend to join in on your weekend fun.

Pets, especially new pets, also require an investment of time. They need to be trained, which can involve scratched-up furniture and the occasional "accident" on the living room rug as they are becoming house trained. They need to learn your house rules — do not bite the baby, do not steal food from the table, and do not pounce on the children. Helping your pet successfully become a part of your house requires you to spend the time teaching and enforcing your house rules just as you have to teach these rules to your children. If you are busy trying to keep your toddler from flushing all his or her toys down the toilet, the prospect of also house training your new puppy might seem overwhelming.

## How often are you out of town?

If you travel a lot for business or take numerous vacations, a pet might not fit into your lifestyle. Pets require food, water, and attention, which means that if you are going out of town, you need to make arrangements for your pet to have all of those things. Pet-sitters and kennels can be expensive and certainly will not give your pet the one-on-one time with its owner that it craves. Traveling with a pet can come with plenty of challenges, including high costs and the added difficulty of finding pet-friendly accommodations.

This does not mean that taking family vacations or going on business trips precludes the possibility of pet ownership. Plenty of families manage to have pets and the occasional trip to Disney World with no problem. But if travel is an essential part of your life and you want to have a pet, it is important to know that it is not always easy to merge the two.

## Can you handle a pet and your child?

Your child may be calm and sweet now, but in about six months he or she might be insanity-on-wheels, racing around the house and getting into trouble in every room that is not gated off. You have a sweet 9-year-old daughter now, but in just four years, she could be a teenager with a bad attitude.

Keep this in mind since you are making a big commitment if you get a pet. A cat, for instance, has an average lifespan of 15–17 years, meaning that if you adopt a kitten when your daughter is 4, you may still have that same cat when your daughter graduates from college. Getting a pet means that you are willing to take on the responsibility of owning that pet, even as your responsibilities for your child change in ways you cannot necessarily prepare for or anticipate.

## Do you have any health concerns?

Allergies may factor into your decision. Obviously, if your spouse is allergic to cats or your son sneezes every time he is around a dog, a pet might not work in your household. Once you make up your mind what kind of pet you want, it is important for all members of your family to spend time around that pet to test for allergic reactions. Keep in mind that different breeds can cause different reactions, so your daughter may be just fine with your neighbor's poodle but suffer from allergies whenever she is in the room with a border collie. It is a good idea to make sure your child has an opportunity to spend time around a pet before you bring it home for good so that you can check for allergic reactions.

## How stable is your life?

If you know you are looking ahead to significant changes in the near future — having a new baby, taking a new job, planning a big move, or finishing a graduate degree — it might be wiser to wait a few months to add a pet to your family. Not only will sudden changes be confusing for your pet, but these changes also take up your time, limiting your ability to care for and bond with your new pet.

As parents, we all have "one of those days" now and again, but if you are consistently overwhelmed by your daily responsibilities of parenting and work, it may be a good idea to wait before getting a pet. As your children get older and are better able to do things for themselves, you may find that you have more time and space to devote to a pet. If you are already feeling like your daily duties are too much, adding more to the mix is probably not a great idea.

## Are you allowed to have a pet?

If you rent, your lease may spell out what kinds of pets you can and cannot have. If you want to get a pet that is prohibited by your lease, it is imperative that you talk with your landlord and not get the pet if it is forbidden. If you do get the pet in spite of your landlord's refusal and lease provisions and your landlord finds out, he or she can force you to get rid of the pet or move out; neither of which is good for your family. If your current living situation does not allow you to have pets, wait until you are living somewhere that does permit pets. If you are renting and allowed to have pets, keep in mind that when you move, you will have to find another place that allows pets, which can somewhat limit your options.

Even if you own your home, some neighborhoods and cities have rules prohibiting specific pets, such as pit bulls, Rottweilers, or exotic pets, such as reptiles. Some also have regulations limiting ownership of loud animals. Be sure you are aware of any such regulations in your area before choosing a pet.

## Worth the Wait

If your family has experienced any of these things in the past six months or if you anticipate experiencing these things in the next six months, seriously consider waiting to get a pet:

- Divorce
- Marriage
- Change in living arrangements, such as moving to a new home
- Pregnancy or a new baby arriving
- Changes at work, including new duties, longer hours, or job loss
- Financial concerns
- Death of a family member
- Frequent travel
- Disagreement within your family about whether to get a pet
- Children leaving or returning home

- Ill or hospitalized parents who need care
- Death or loss of another family pet
- Significant health problems in your immediate family

Though none of these factors means your family absolutely should not adopt a pet, they do indicate a temporary lack of stability that might not make it the best time to bring home an animal.

## Expectations

Once you have determined that your lifestyle is conducive to pet ownership, it is time to think about why you want a pet and what you expect from having a pet. Answering these questions can help you determine whether you really are ready to take on the responsibilities of pet ownership or if your dream is not quite ready to become a reality yet.

## Who is the pet for?

You may feel strongly that Jane and Jack should not grow up without a dog, but maybe Jane and Jack seem to have no interest in most pets or are frightened when the neighbor's friendly dog gets a little too close. Or, maybe Jane has been obsessed with kittens for so long that you finally give in, even though you do not really want a pet.

It is OK to get a pet because your whole family wants one; it is not OK to get a pet for your children if you do not really want to have a pet. Be clear about your motives and involve everyone in the family in the discussion. You should not get a pet unless your whole family is in agreement on wanting a pet. Getting a pet that you do not really want is a recipe for disaster, and animal shelters are full of pets that just "did not work out." Be sure you really want a pet — and the responsibilities that come with it — before you make your final decision.

## Who will take care of the pet?

Your child may be pleading for a puppy, but it is the parents who end up shouldering the burden of housebreaking, rainy-night walks, and veterinarian bills — even if your child insists he or she will take care of it. Children get excited about cuddling and playtime and can romanticize the feeding and grooming right out of the picture. Parents, however, are the ones who end up doing most of the pet care, so understand that fact before you bring home a pet. Do not choose a pet if you are not 100 percent willing to take care of 100 percent of its responsibilities. Assume that your child will have no role whatsoever in the care and feeling of your new pet — would you be willing to adopt it under those conditions? Ideally, and most likely, your child will pitch in on some help, but to be sound in your decision, you should adopt a pet only if you are willing to assume full responsibility for it.

## What will having a pet be like?

It is easy to focus on the fun parts of pet ownership while ignoring the challenges. For instance, you may think about how exciting and soothing it will be to watch your tropical fish swim in their aquarium, and you may congratulate yourself on choosing a relatively low-maintenance pet that does not require house-training; but, be sure that you also take into account the day-to-day reality of owning your pet: Most fish tanks need to be cleaned once a week, which can involve the messy process of putting fish in temporary homes while you clean the tank. Freshwater fish need to be fed twice a day or on their particular feeding schedule — even if you are on vacation. Aquariums need to be located in safe places where curious toddlers cannot reach inside them or knock them over. The pH balance of water in the aquarium needs to be checked regularly.

There are many wonderful things about having pets, and it is nice to focus on those parts of pet ownership. But it is just as important to focus on the realities of caring for a pet. Chapters 3–7 of this book will explain the major responsibilities associated with the most common types of family pets and offer age-specific recommendations for how children can be involved in their care so that you know exactly what duties you are signing up for in adopting a particular pet.

# Space

Some pets need a lot of space and other pets just a little, but all pets need the right kind of space. Make sure you have it before you make the decision to get a pet.

## What kind of indoor space do you have?

Indoor animals need to have comfortable, quiet space to eat and sleep. If your pet spends most of its time in a cage or crate, make sure you have enough space to comfortably house it. If a pet needs sunlight or to be away from sunlight — as some fish or lizards do — make sure your home has enough room to give your pet the space it needs without interfering with your living areas. You will also want to make sure that the cage is easily accessible to you and other caretakers but safely located away from very young children who might harm the pet in their desire to love it.

Pets who roam free inside need a designated feeding area and a space to eliminate waste, whether that is a litter box, a trip outside, or a spot in their cage. This should be an area that the animal can easily access without assistance but one that is hard for little hands to reach. Some animals can become aggressive if their feeding is interrupted, so you will want to make sure you have space to set up their eating area away from a high-traffic area of your home.

If you are away from home during the day because of work or school, make sure you have a comfortable, safe space for your pet to stay. You will want to make sure you have an area that you can pet proof so that your pet cannot get into potentially harmful substances or damage anything valuable. Do not assume a garage or basement is automatically the best place to house your pet, since these areas can be full of potential hazards. If you plan to have a kennel or crate for your pet, make sure you have an appropriate space to put it.

## What kind of outdoor space do you have?

Many pets stay indoors and do just fine. There are large dogs that call urban apartments — with no outdoor spaces of their own — home, and as long as their owners are willing to walk them regularly, the dog hardly minds.

Still, an outdoor area can be a nice spot for a pet, especially a dog. If you plan to let your pet out in your yard unleashed, you will want to make sure that your yard has a fence or similar boundary so that your dog stays safe and cannot race out into a road or bother a neighbor. If you live in a neighborhood with a homeowners' association, check into its pet covenants: Some have strict rules about pets left outside and audible barking, which may affect your pet decisions. If you are planning to put up a fence or other barrier to make your backyard safe for your pet, make sure that your plans mesh with your neighborhood and city ordinances.

## 10 Best Cities for Pet Lovers

You do not have to live in one of these pet-friendly spots to bring home a pet for your family, but these areas combine green space and good weather that make many pets — and their owners — happy. (This list considered factors including access to veterinary care, population density, and local pet laws

in determining the top 10 cities for pet lovers.)

1. Ellicott City, Maryland
2. Rocky Point, New York
3. Auburn, Alabama
4. Butte, Montana
5. Yankton, South Dakota
6. Lewiston, Idaho
7. Glasgow, Kentucky
8. Aiken, South Carolina
9. Flower Mound, Texas
10. Wolf Trap, Virginia

*Source:* U.S. News & World Report (**www. usnews.com**), August 2009

# Previous Experience

If you have never had a pet, it is hard to exactly understand the kinds of responsibilities pet ownership will entail — in much of the same way that it is hard for people who have never been parents to understand the responsibilities of having a child. Considering your previous experience with specific kinds of pets as well as pets in general can help clue you in to how prepared you are for pet ownership — individually and as a family.

## Have you had a pet before?

If you had a beloved pet growing up, do not assume that you know everything about caring for that particular pet; you may be surprised by how much pet-care responsibility your parents assumed (you can remind your own children of this fact some day). Being partially responsible for a pet, though, does give you a clearer perspective of what pet ownership entails for that particular kind of pet. You do not have to have owned a pet in the past to become a successful pet owner. If you are an inexperienced pet owner, you might consider starting with a lower-maintenance family pet, such as a bird or fish, instead of pets that require more care and expense, like cats and dogs. Or you might have your heart set on a dog and be willing to take on all the responsibilities that requires. If you are a new, first-time pet owner, it might be smart to enroll in a pet care class to learn the basics of what your new pet will need to be healthy and happy before you commit. Many local humane societies and animal protection programs offer these types of classes.

## Has your spouse had a pet before?

If you grew up with the responsibility of caring for three cats, but your partner really wants a puppy because he or she never had one as a child, be aware that he or she may not fully understand the responsibilities of pet ownership. Again, being new to pet ownership does not mean that you are not ready to have a pet, but it can impact what kind of pet is best for you. Spend time with someone who already owns the kind of pet you are considering, and talk with him or her about the pros and cons of caring for that pet. If your spouse owned a pet previously, he or she can be a good resource for filling you in on some of the details of owning a particular pet.

## Has your family had a pet before?

This can be a hard question to face. Perhaps you had a dog when you brought your first baby home from the hospital, but after a few months, realized you could not handle the demands of a new child and an active dog. Maybe you adopted a kitten from a supermarket shelter lineup only to realize that your 2-year-old was not careful enough to keep the tiny kitten safe. If you had a pet in the past that did not work out, be very honest with yourself about what did not work and why it did not work. How are things different now? If your life has not changed, the problem that made that pet unsuccessful is likely to still exist; you may need to consider your decision more carefully.

# Cost

There is no doubt about it: Pets are expensive. Committing to pet ownership is a commitment to regular expenditures, so it is important to choose a pet that will work with your family's budget.

Here are some of the costs that pet owners incur in adopting and keeping their pet healthy:

- Adoption fee or purchase price
- Vaccinations (if not included in adoption fee or price)
- Spay or neuter surgery (if not included in adoption fee or price)
- Food and treats
- Feeding supplies, such as bowls, food scoops, and water dispensers
- Collar
- Leash
- Crate, cage, or kennel (larger and fancier will be more expensive)
- Safety gates to block off areas of your home or yard
- Toys
- License fees
- Identification tags
- Teeth cleaning
- Grooming
- Health care and checkups
- Boarding or pet-sitting when needed
- Travel items and travel expenses

The following chart, "A Quick Look," shows the one-time and recurring costs associated with owning some of the most common pets. Of course, there are costs associated with different areas and specific pets that may not be reflected in the information in this chart, and the purchase price will vary depending on breed. As it clearly indicates, the cost of owning a pet goes far beyond the initial adoption fee. Be sure your family can afford the adoption fee or purchase price, as well as the ongoing expenses of pet ownership before you bring a pet into your family. (Costs for adopting small pets, birds, or fish are not included because these animals are not commonly available for adoption. If you are committed to adopting and have your heart set on one of these pets, you will probably have more luck with a local rescue group than with an animal shelter.)

| A QUICK LOOK | | | | | |
|---|---|---|---|---|---|
| Pet | Cost to adopt | Cost to purchase | Estimated annual vet costs | Estimated monthly food costs | Estimated life span |
| Dog | $25–$100 | $50+ | $200–$250 | $20+ | 10–20 years |
| Cat | $25–$100 | $25+ | $100–$150 | $30+ | 14–20 years |
| Goldfish | n/a | $.75–$3 | $0 | $1 | 2–3 years |
| Parrot | n/a | $100–$500 | $100–$300 | $20–$30 | 40+ years |
| Hamster | n/a | $4–$20 | $0 | $5 | 3–4 years |
| Gerbil | n/a | $10–$35 | $50–$75 | $15 | 5–8 years |

## Your Child

One of the most challenging parts of deciding to bring a pet into your family is figuring out when your child is ready for a pet to join the family. It is an important question, since your child is an integral part of your family life. Answering these questions should help you determine whether your child is ready for a pet.

## How much time has your child spent around animals?

Does your child love Grandma's pet cat and look forward to visiting the neighbor's hamsters, or does her closest relationship with an animal come from her favorite book?

If your child regularly spends time with other people's animals, you have an excellent opportunity to observe her interest in animals. Does he or she make a beeline for Grandma's cat the minute she walks in the door? Does he or she ignore or avoid animals at other people's homes? The more time your child has spent with animals, the better sense you can get of his or her comfort and behavior around them. If your child has not had much opportunity to spend time with animals, her or she may need a lot of coaching to learn how to behave appropriately, and it might be wiser to opt for an animal that is not easily injured and that does not need specialized care.

## How does your child react to strange animals?

If you are strolling through the park and your son spots a dog on a leash, does he rush to lavish the dog with love? Do you have to remind your child to wait for the owner's permission to approach strange dogs, or does he or she huddle up against your leg in terror when a friendly dog approaches?

Ideally, your child should be excited around animals but have enough self-control to wait for permission before touching them and to be gentle with them when he or she does touch them. If your child is afraid of most animals or gets overexcited around them, you will want to think carefully about whether he or she needs to develop a little more maturity before you add a pet to the family.

## Has your child asked for a pet?

Some children forget that pets even exist unless the pet in question is right in front of them. Others are obsessed with puppies and will read every book about puppies, watch every movie about puppies, and spend most of their waking hours talking about puppies and asking when your family can get one.

If your child is not interested in a pet, that does not mean you absolutely should not adopt one, but it does mean that you should acknowledge that the pet you are adopting is going to be more your pet than a family pet. Children may get closer to pets as they gets older, making it more of a family pet, but there is no guarantee that will happen. And wanting a pet does not necessarily mean your child is ready for one, but it can be an indicator that a pet may be right for your family.

## How is your child with smaller children?

The way older children treat younger children can be a good indicator of how they will do with a pet. If they are generally calm and considerate and respond well to reminders to be calm, they will likely do well with a pet. If they get annoyed easily or play too rough with the little ones, they will probably act similarly with a pet. This does not mean a pet is an absolute no-go, but it can be a sign to tread carefully with your pet choice.

## How much free time does your child have?

Like your own schedule, your child's schedule cannot include a pet unless there is room in it for a pet. If your child has afternoons and weekends packed with baseball practice, piano lessons, and other activities, now is probably not the best time to get a pet. But if your child has at least one free hour a day — not including meals or homework time — a pet can be a possibility for your family.

If your child does not seem ready for a pet right now, do not despair. Children mature quickly and often suddenly, so reconsider your child's readiness every six months or so. You will be surprised by how much your child and your family's overall pet readiness can change in a short time. If having a pet is important to your family, the right time will come, and you will be glad you waited for that right time.

## 5 Signs Your Family is Ready for a Pet

If you agree with the five statements below, your family is probably ready to take on the responsibility of a pet. If not, you may be wise to wait a little longer.

1.  **We know what kind of pet we want.** There is a big difference between vaguely deciding to adopt a pet and taking the time to learn about a specific animal and its needs. Doing the research to find a pet that is right for your family instead of just dreaming of a family pet suggests that you are ready to take the plunge.

2.  **We can afford to take care of our pet.** It is not just about buying food, which can be pricey enough. Pets also need grooming and feeding supplies, regular visits to the veterinarian, and pet gear like crates or leashes. Some need regular medications. If you have analyzed your family finances and determined that you can afford a pet, you are more likely to become successful pet owners.

3. **We understand that playtime is only part of the time.** Yes, having a pet is fun, and playtime can be a blast. But a good pet owner understands that there is a lot more to having a pet than just playing and is ready to take responsibility for the parts that are less fun and just as important, such as vaccinations, grooming, and discipline.

4. **We are ready to take our time.** You understand that you might not find the right pet on your first scouting expedition, and you are OK with that. You want more than a quick pet fix — you are willing to wait for the right pet to come along.

5. **We understand that being pet owners is a long-term commitment.** Adding another member to your family is a lifetime commitment, whether your new member is a human or an animal. Some pets have long a life span that will continue after your children are grown up and on their own. A good pet owner chooses a pet knowing that the choice has long-term ramifications.

# Chapter 2

Choosing the Right Pet

N ow that you have decided it is the right time to bring a pet into your family, it is time decide which pet is right for you and your family. Below are a series of exercises to help you evaluate what kind of pet is best for your family. Each quiz evaluates your perfect pet based on the information in the previous chapter. At the end of the chapter, you can determine your ideal family pet by ranking the factors in order of their importance to you and choosing the pet that resonates best with your family's particular needs.

## Lifestyle

The purpose of these questions is to help you determine how much time and energy your family has to devote to a pet. What kind of pet works best with your family's lifestyle? Answer the following questions to find out:

1.  On most weekdays, I am:
    a.  At work
    b.  Working from home
    c.  At home, taking care of the house

2.  On most weekdays, my spouse or partner is:
    a.  At his or her/her place of work
    b.  Working from home
    c.  At home, taking care of the house

3.  My family travels:
    a.  A couple of big trips and a few weekend getaways each year
    b.  Three or four times a year, including the occasional weekend getaway
    c.  Once or twice a year at most

4.  My schedule is:
    a.  Jam-packed: I cannot remember the last time I had a lazy weekend
    b.  Busy, but with plenty of downtime
    c.  Fairly calm: Hectic weekends are the exception, not the rule

5.  I expect to move:
    a.  Within the next six months
    b.  Sometime in the next couple of years
    c.  I have no plans to move

6.  I am planning to have another child:
    a.  Soon: I am pregnant or actively trying to get pregnant or adopt

    b.  Eventually, but I do not plan to start trying for a while

    c.  My family is perfect as it is

7.   Does anyone in my family have pet allergies?

    a.  Yes

    b.  I do not know

    c.  No

8.   Am I allowed to have pets in my current home?

    a.  No

    b.  I do not know

    c.  Yes

## If you answered:

**Mostly A's:** Your busy schedule and fast-paced life is best suited for a low-maintenance pet that requires little daily upkeep, such as a fish *(Chapter 6)* or hamster *(Chapter 7)*.

**Mostly B's:** Your life has room for a pet, but since you have a busy schedule already, it is worth considering how much time you want to devote to a pet. If you are willing to sacrifice your already limited free time for an animal, you can consider a higher-maintenance pet, such as a dog *(Chapter 3)*, cat *(Chapter 4)*, or bird *(Chapter 5)*. If you are hoping to keep a little free time for other activities, a lower-maintenance pet such as a fish or gerbil might be a better fit for your family right now.

**Mostly C's:** Your life is settled, and you have plenty of time for bringing in another member to the family. You can comfortably

45

choose a pet such as a dog, cat, or bird that requires an hour or more of care each day.

## Your schedule

If your home is empty during the day while you are at work and your children are in school or day care, it could be a lonely place for a pet that requires companionship. If you decide to get a dog or cat, you will need to figure out what your pet will do during the day while you are not home. If you are home all day, you may enjoy having a highly socialized pet, such as a bird, dog, or cat, which can offer companionship during the time when you are at home.

Your family's travel habits also matter when it comes to choosing a pet. If you like the spontaneity of spur-of-the-moment travel, consider what you will do with your animal when you travel. Will you take your animal with you? If so, you will need to choose an animal that travels well and one that is comfortable in planes, trains, and hotel rooms, as well as tracking down accommodations that accept pets. Will you leave your animal at home? If so, you will need to be aware of boarding or pet-sitting costs. A low-maintenance animal like a fish or a gerbil can probably be left at home and checked on by a neighbor or friend, but higher-maintenance animals like dogs and cats cannot be left alone for long periods of time. You will need to make more intensive arrangements for their care, whether it is enlisting the help of a cooperative neighbor or booking space at a kennel.

If your schedule is already full, it is probably not wise to add a pet that requires a lot of daily care time. *For a list of estimated daily care times for common family pets, see the "Timing Is Everything" chart in this chapter.* For instance, dogs and cats need more than an hour of care each day, including feeding, playing, and grooming time. If you do not have extra time in your schedule, trying to create that extra time is likely to be difficult. Your family might do better with a pet like a goldfish that requires only a few minutes of active care each day. If you have plenty of extra time and like the idea of dedicating some of it to your new pet, a higher-maintenance dog, cat, or bird might be a good option.

Some animals are more move-friendly than others, so if you have a move in your immediate future but want a pet right now, consider a pet that has a home within your home. Pets like dogs and cats can have a hard time adjusting to a new home, but gerbils and hamsters that spend most of their time in a cage or fish that spend most of its time in a bowl or aquarium can change houses or apartments without much fuss.

Consider your family, too. Taking on a dog or cat when you know you have a new baby on the way might be a problem in the making: As a parent, you know how time-consuming that first year with a new baby can be, so be careful not to optimistically overestimate how much time you will have for a pet when a new baby arrives. If your family is still growing, consider a lower-maintenance pet until you feel confident you can handle the demands of a higher-maintenance one.

Finally, think about the age of your pet. If you have young children, consider whether you are willing to potty train and house train at the same time, and how much obedience training you are willing to do so your new pet will not play rough with your children. If your children are young and your time and patience is limited but you really want a dog or cat, consider bringing home an older animal rather than a puppy or a kitten. An animal that is already trained and housebroken can make having a higher-maintenance pet much more feasible for younger families.

Other things to consider: If you are active, look for a pet that can participate in activities like running and playing ball with your family. If your family is quieter, choose a pet that enjoys spending quiet time at home, like a cat or fish.

The following chart shows the average amount of care time the following common pets need each day. Knowing how much time you have available to care for a pet as well as how much care a particular pet needs can help you make a good pet choice for your family.

| TIMING IS EVERYTHING | |
|---|---|
| *Pet* | *Average Daily Care Time* |
| Dog | 2–4 hours |
| Cat | 1–2 hours |
| Goldfish | 3–5 minutes |
| Parrot | 1 hour |
| Hamster | 30 minutes |
| Gerbil | 30 minutes |

## Expectations

These questions are designed to help you find a pet. For each set of statements, choose the one that is the most true for you.

**A. I am willing to spend more than an hour a day caring for a pet.**
**B. I am not willing to spend more than an hour a day caring for a pet.**

Be honest with yourself about how much extra time you have and are willing to spend taking care of something else. Remember: A pet is a full-time commitment, including days when you are tired, stressed out, or busy, and the ultimate responsibility for making sure your pet is healthy and taken care of is yours, not your child's.

**A. I want a pet that is playful and interactive.**
**B. I want a pet that is calm and often inactive.**

A playful pet will always be up for fun activity, but you will have to spend lots of time interacting with it to keep a playful pet truly happy. Calmer pets are happier to observe than to play, but they will not whine if you are too busy to play with them during busy times. Playful pets include dogs, cats and small pets like gerbils and hamsters. Calmer, more sedentary pets include birds and fish.

**A. I want a pet that will be physically affectionate and cuddly.**
**B. I want a pet that does not need much physical affection.**

Though there are exceptions within breeds, most dogs and small pets are physically affectionate and enjoy lots of physical contact. Cats like physical affection but also like alone time so may not always be willing to cuddle when you want to. Birds are affectionate and social but not cuddly in the same way that dogs, cats, and small animals are. Fish require essentially no physical contact.

**A. I want a pet that my child can help with by sharing some of the responsibility.**
**B. I want a pet that can be kept safe from my child.**

Dogs and cats are good animals for children to learn to care for because their larger size makes them sturdier and easier for children to engage — especially if you bypass puppies and kittens and opt for older animals that are full-grown and well socialized. If you want a pet that your child can only access when you are there, caged or contained pets are a good option since your child can play with them and care for them only when you are supervising. Birds can be fragile, and if you are worried about your child harming your pet in his or her zealousness, it might be wise to save a pet bird for when your child understands the importance of being gentle with animals.

**A. I do not mind a little wear and tear on my house because of my pet.**

**B. I would prefer that our pet not scratch or harm our home and furnishings.**

Do not get a dog or cat unless you are prepared for some scratched up furniture and the occasional knocked over vase. Young dogs and cats are the most likely to add wear and tear to your home since they are still learning the house rules, but even older dogs and cats will occasionally get too excited or startled and cause household chaos. If you want a pet that will not bring any wear and tear to your home, look for a pet that comes in a self-contained habitat, such as fish, birds, or other small pets.

**A. I want a pet that will communicate with me.**

**B. Hearing my pet's voice is not important to me.**

Dogs, cats, and birds are verbally precocious and can have "conversations" with their owners. Children may enjoy repeating their sounds, and parents may appreciate that these pets can be verbally responsive. Fish and other small animals are generally quiet and do not do much verbalizing.

**A. I prefer a pet that does not mind being left on its own for longer periods of time.**
**B. I am comfortable with a pet that needs daily attention.**

Fish and many small animals are fine when left to their own devices for long stretches of time as long they have access to food and water. Other pets will not thrive without daily contact and playtime.

**A. I do not mind spending time training my pet.**
**B. I would prefer my pet to need minimal training.**

Age is partly the issue here: If you are not ready to take on the job of housebreaking and obedience training, do not adopt a kitten, a puppy, or a very young bird. Older dogs, cats, and birds are less likely to require intensive training, especially if the animals are well socialized. Fish and other small animals require almost no training even in the very early days.

**A. I am willing to make many changes in my home for a pet.**
**B. I am willing to make a few changes in my home for a pet.**
**C. I would rather not make any changes in my home for a pet.**

If you would rather keep the lay of the land at home exactly as it is, your best bet is a fish or small caged pet that spends most of its time comfortably in its own habitat container. Dogs and cats require a little accommodation, including: designated feeding areas, a litter area for cats, the occasional baby gate to protect a particular room, and other relatively minor space needs. Birds require the most accommodation, requiring the removal of many common household items that can affect their more delicate systems, making them a better choice for families who are willing to make adjustments at home to welcome their new pet.

## Space

Use these questions to help you determine what type of pet your current living situation is best suited for.

1. Our new pet will be spending most of its time:
   a. Indoors
   b. Outdoors
   c. Both indoors and outdoors

If your pet will be spending time outside — especially if some of that time will be with minimal supervision — it is vital that your outdoor space be secure. Dogs and cats (the pets most likely to be allowed out on their own) are very agile and can slip through cracks in and under fences, leap off decks and balconies, and generally exploit any chink in your home's outdoor armor, so do not take on an outdoor pet unless you truly have the secure space to accommodate it.

2. We can accommodate (mark all that apply):
   a. A separate pet feeding area
   b. A pet waste area
   c. Pet toys, pillows, and other gear
   d. A playful animal that needs space to roam
   e. Very little extra space

If you decide to adopt a cat or a dog, you will need to have a permanent, secure feeding area for your pet that younger children cannot easily access and interfere with. A cat also needs a waste area for a litter box; obviously, this should be in an area where younger children cannot get into it because of health issues related to handling fecal matter. Unless you are willing to sacrifice your furniture, you will also need space for scratching posts and a few cat toys. Dogs who spend their time inside may need a crate for nighttime and for when they are at home alone. Depending on the size of your dog, a crate can require a tremendous amount of space, so be sure your home has enough space to accommodate an appropriately sized crate. Cats, dogs, and birds also need space to roam to stay healthy and happy. A large pet in cramped quarters may end up unhealthy and unhappy. Fish need containers, which can range from very small to enormous: Know how much space you have before choosing a fish and its accessories. Small pets usually do not need much more space than their cages, though these can vary in size, too.

## The Do's and Do Not's of Choosing a Pet

*Do* spend time researching and visiting pets to find one that is right for your family.

*Do not* get a pet on impulse because it is "cute."

*Do* choose a pet whose needs you understand and know you can accommodate.

*Do not* choose a pet whose needs you know nothing about and assume you can make it work.

*Do* let your child participate in choosing the family pet.

*Do not* choose a pet unless you are willing and able to do all the caretaking it requires, even if the pet is going to be your child's.

# Cost

Pets can be very expensive and most require an initial expenditure that is not insignificant. You are not just buying a dog: You are also buying that dog's first vaccinations and spay/neuter operation (usually included in the adoption fees), its feeding equipment, crate, food supply, leash, and other equipment. The same is true for a pet like a fish: In addition to the cost of the fish, you have to buy the fish tank, water filter, heater, aquarium rocks, water conditioner, plants and other tank supplies. These first costs can be surprisingly high, so it is important to know what you can actually afford. If it is important to you to get a pet but you cannot afford one right now, you can start a pet savings fund to save money so that you can afford your pet.

This section will help you to determine which pet is the best economic fit for your family. Keep in mind that these costs are based on national averages, which means depending on your pet's particular diet and needs, you may pay more or less per year for your pet than these numbers suggest.

1.  How much money am I willing to invest in start-up costs? (Purchase price, essential gear for feeding, housing and grooming, and one-time costs like vaccinations)
    a.  More than $1,000
    b.  Around $700
    c.  Around $150
    d.  Less than $100

If you answered A: You can afford to adopt any of the pets covered in this book.

**If you answered B**: You can afford to adopt a cat or a bird, as well as any of the other less expensive pets below. You could spend more than this, depending on the breed of animal you choose and what gear you purchase for it, but you should plan to spend at least this much.

**If you answered C**: You can afford to bring home a fish, as well as any of the other less expensive pets below. While you can certainly spend more than $150 on a high-end tank and accessories for your fish, you can also spend much less for a single goldfish in a bowl if you forgo the fancy aquarium. Falling somewhere in the middle of extravagant to simple, you can get a small tank of fish with some plants and accessories for $150.

**If you answered D**: Your budget does not leave you much room to buy an expensive pet that needs a lot of equipment, so consider one of the smaller pets: Guinea pigs, rats, hamsters, mice, gerbils, and some lizards and other reptiles are affordable because their initial costs are lower than those for some other animals.

2. How much money am I willing to spend on my pet each month? (Food, grooming, toys, and occasional vet visits)
   a. $120 or more
   b. $75 or more
   c. $25 or more
   d. $20 or more
   e. $2 or more

**If you answered A**: Dogs are the most expensive pets to maintain from month to month. Grooming and food costs combined with heartworm medication can easily come to $120 per month for your pet dog. Larger dogs that eat more food may be even more expensive, and it is possible to have a smaller dog that might not cost as much. Dogs with long hair or hair that needs a particular kind of regular grooming may incur more in grooming fees. You can afford a pet dog for $120 a month, as well as any of the other less expensive pets below.

**If you answeRed B**: For $75 each month, you can afford to take on the responsibility of a pet cat or any of the less expensive pets listed below. In addition to food, cats need regular grooming.

**If you answeRed C**: You can afford to take on the cost of a small animal, such as a hamster or gerbil, or a reptile, as well as any of the less expensive pets listed below. Though the initial costs for a small pet like a hamster or a reptile can be fairly low, their monthly upkeep is more expensive than you might think because of food and cage maintenance.

**If you answeRed D**: You can afford the monthly expenses of caring for a bird. Birds have a high initial cost since they can be expensive and require specific gear, but once you have made that initial purchase, their monthly upkeep is reasonable.

**If you answeRed E**: You are better off getting a fish. They are the most-affordable pet on a daily basis and need little more than food to stay healthy and well cared for.

Again, if you have your heart set on a particular pet that your current budget cannot support, create a pet savings fund that will let you save the money you need to get the pet you want. If you have a substantial amount of money to spend on your pet's adoption or purchase but little money to allocate to monthly pet expenses, consider purchasing a less-expensive pet and setting the money you have saved aside to help cover the monthly expenses. If the pet you want your family to have does not work well with your budget right now, there are ways to be creative with what you have or to save money to make the pet you want a possibility for your family.

## Your Child

One of the most important parts of choosing a pet for your family is determining which pet is right for your child. Use these questions to help you make the smart choice.

1. When it comes to other people's pets, my child:
   a. Cannot wait to get his or her hands on them and needs frequent reminders to be gentle
   b. Would rather look than touch
   c. Is gentle with them and uses a soft voice

If your child is a grabber who needs help remembering to be gentle with animals, be careful. Ideally, adopt a larger animal that has experience with children, since many animals will react with biting and scratching when they feel afraid or threatened. Another alternative is to choose a pet that your children can only interact with when you are there to supervise, or to select a pet that does not need physical interaction. If your child prefers to keep his or her distance from most animals, he or she might enjoy the company of a bird. Birds are fascinating to watch and fun to verbalize with, but most are fairly fragile and should not be handled too much by young or careless children. Fish and reptiles are also a good choice for children who prefer to interact with animals through observation. If your child is used to being around animals and knows that a gentle voice and gentle touch are important, you can consider getting a pet such as a dog or cat that will regularly interact with your child or a small creature such as a guinea pig or hamster that your child can access on his or her own.

2. When it comes to cleanliness, my child:
   a. Often washes his or her hands without prompting
   b. Washes his or her hands if reminded
   c. Could go for days without washing his or her hands

If you have a child who is truly fastidious about keeping clean, a reptile that can carry bacteria such as salmonella is a possibility. In fact, a child who remembers to wash his or her hands can welcome pretty much any pet you can think of. Only a truly fastidious child should adopt a reptile. The slight risk of salmonella these animals carry means that it is imperative your child wash her hands every time she handles the pet, its cage, or any of its belongings. Children who are generally pretty good about washing their hands will do fine with most pets: Washing hands is a good idea after petting your dog or cat or handling your small pet, but forgetting to do it now and again is not likely to cause a health crisis. Still, children who never clean their hands should avoid pets that get handled and opt instead for look-but-do-not-touch-pets such as fish.

3. When it comes to the amount of work involved in caring for a pet, my child:

    a. Knows the score: He or she has helped care for pets and been involved in some aspects of feeding, training, and house training for the pet you are considering

    b. Has a general idea of the work involved in caring for a pet but does not know much about the specifics

    c. Does not have a clue: In his or her mind, it is all fun and cuddles

There is not really a right answer to this question. Some children who have no idea of the work involved in caring for a puppy may get so excited about their new pet that they tackle their responsibilities with delighted success, while children who enthusiastically take care of a neighbor's pet may have little interest in tackling responsibility for their own pet. Still, it is smart to encourage children to participate in care-taking duties for your family pet early in the process, so take your child's knowledge into account as you are choosing a pet. If your child has had successful experiences with a neighbor's gerbil, those experiences may make him or her more inclined toward that animal as a pet. If your child hated your mother's yapping dog that stayed with you while she was on a cruise, he or she may be less excited about having a dog.

    4. How much time does my child have to spend with a pet?

        a. He or she has a busy schedule, but it includes at least an hour of free time at home each day

        b. He or she is so busy she barely has time to eat dinner most nights, between schoolwork and after-school activities

        c. He or she has plenty of free time — possibly too much

It is important to choose a pet that your family will have time to enjoy. If your child truly has an hour free each day, almost any pet is a possibility. Just be sure that free hour is one he or she is willing to give up for pet care. If it is not, you may want to avoid pets that need a lot of maintenance and attention and choose a pet that enjoys companionship and independence. If your child's schedule is already completely full, do not introduce a pet who needs a lot of attention — it is a recipe for disaster. Instead, choose a low-maintenance pet, which can satisfy your need for a pet without a lot of effort. If your child has lots of time, a dog or cat might be a good idea, but do not discount the appeal of a small hamster. These furry little creatures love playtime and are endlessly entertaining; some even make glad whistling sounds when they hear their owners coming. For children who want a pet to play with, these kinds of small pets can be a great option.

5. My child is:
   a. Younger than 6 years old
   b. Between 6 and 10
   c. Older than 10

Obviously, children vary in terms of their maturity levels, and it is possible to have an incredibly mature and responsible 4-year-old who would do well with a delicate animal or an immature 12-year-old who cannot remember to play calmly with a puppy. In general, though, if you have a child younger than 6, you should avoid getting an easily injured pet unless you can be sure that your child will only be able to get close to the pet when you are directly supervising him or her. Young children can easily injure small creatures without meaning to do so. Also avoid adopting a young, untrained animal. Not only is it easy for a child to injure smaller animals, it is also likely that these animals could injure your child by scratching or biting. Toddlers and puppies are both prone to loving someone until it hurts.

If you have a child between 6 and 10 years old, there is a good chance your child can handle most pets. This is a good age to adopt a young pet because most children of this age have the patience and understanding to cope with a puppy's antics and the responsibility to be gentle with smaller creatures. Dogs and cats are good choices for this age group. For the same reasons puppies and kittens are possible for youngsters this age, small pets like gerbils and guinea pigs are good options. Children between 6 and 10 years old are able to enjoy the antics of these little creatures and to treat them gently and carefully. Children this age also enjoy fish and can enjoy watching fish interact in an aquarium. Children older than 10 can handle unusual pets, such as reptiles well, in addition to the pets mentioned above.

6.  Does my child have any allergies?
    a.  Yes
    b.  No

If your child is prone to serious allergies, it might be in your family's best interest to choose a pet that does not tend to cause allergic reactions, such as a bird, fish, or reptile.

Once you have completed this chapter, you should have an idea of what pet is right for your family. You know which factors carry the most weight for your particular family and can use the information from those sections to make a decision that is right for you. The following chapters will make it even easier, as we detail the advantages and challenges of some of the most common household pets and give you a clear idea of what your family can expect when you bring home an animal.

## CASE STUDY: NOT-SO-PICTURE PERFECT

Parents: Jennifer and Andy Peterson
Children: Mallory and Allissa
Myrtle Beach, South Carolina

Andy and Jennifer had pets as kids and were so excited about getting a dog for their girls so that they would have the same experience. The family went to the shelter together one weekend and picked out a gorgeous, golden-coated puppy that looked just like a Golden Retriever. Mallory and Allissa fell completely in love with her, and so did Andy and Jennifer. The girls named her Hanna.

They thought they were prepared for what having a dog would mean, but they were not. Andy was starting a new rotation at work and was not home in the evenings, which left Jennifer to deal with a fussy 4-year-old, a tired 2-year-old, and a needy new puppy all by herself. She was not prepared to shuffle the whole family outside every evening so that Hanna could do her business, and she was not happy about having to clean up the puppy's accidents when she did not make it outside. Allissa was still potty training, and sometimes, between her and Hanna, Jennifer felt like she was surrounded by poop.

Jennifer also did not realize how hard it was going to be to keep Hanna safe from Mallory and Allissa. She had pictured the girls playing with Hanna, but she had forgotten how rough they could be. Even with all my reminders about being gentle, she would come into the living room and see Mallory shaking the puppy or Allissa narrowly missing sitting on it.

It was hard to admit it, but the Peterson family was not ready for a puppy. Andy and Jennifer had been so swept up by all the things that were fun about owning a puppy that they had not considered the practical question of how they would juggle caring for the puppy with taking care of the rest of their lives. They just could not do it — and if they had sat down and thought about it, they probably would have realized it.

They were lucky that they were able to find a home for Hanna with one of Andy's coworkers who had been planning to get a puppy for a long time, but Jennifer still feels guilty that she took on the responsibility of caring for a living creature so completely unprepared. She would encourage any family thinking about getting a pet to be very honest with themselves about what kind of time they have to give to caring for a pet.

When the girls get a little older and their lives settle down, Jennifer would still like to get a dog. But this time she will be a lot more thoughtful about what being a pet owner actually entails.

# Chapter 3

Dogs

## At a Glance

| | |
|---|---|
| **THE BEST PART**............... | Dogs are usually among the most affectionate and playful of pets. |
| **THE BIGGEST CHALLENGE**..... | Dogs need more daily maintenance than many pets, and owners need to have at least an hour a day to dedicate to pet caretaking. |
| **COST**............................ | Usually around $850 or more in start-up costs, including adoption or purchase, initial veterinarian visit, and starter gear, and about $20–$100 monthly for food and maintenance. |
| **NEEDS**........................... | Feeding once or twice daily, a long walk at least once a day, several potty breaks a day, and monthly grooming. |
| **AVERAGE LIFESPAN**............ | 8–15 years (Smaller dogs generally live longer than larger ones.) |

Dogs are one of the first pets most people consider when they talk about getting a pet, which is probably the reason why dogs are the most popular pets in the United States today, according to the American Pet Products Manufacturing Association. It is not hard to see why. Most dogs are very social animals who show affection, communicate with their owners, and see their family as their "pack," creating a strong bond. Classic television is filled with kids and their pet dogs: Timmy and his collie Lassie and Elroy Jetson and his space dog Astro are just a couple of examples. Dogs can be wonderful family pets, but they come with their share of challenges. This chapter will look at adopting a dog and the responsibilities it entails, highlighting some of the advantages and challenges of dog ownership, as well as considering what kind of dogs are best for families and how children can get involved in their pet's care.

## What Your Pet Dog Needs

Compared to other pets, dogs can seem very high maintenance. A dog is usually not a good pet for a family with very limited time and resources. Dogs can live up to 15 years old, making them a long-term investment of time, energy, and money.

### Cost

Expect to pay around $1,000 in start-up costs for your dog. Why so much? In addition to the adoption fee (usually between $25 and $100 but can be higher for some rescue organizations or specific breeds) or purchase price (the average cost to purchase a puppy from a breeder is about $500 and can go as high as $1,500 for dogs trained to compete), you will want to invest in all the gear your new dog needs to be comfortable. This may include:

- A crate, for times your dog will be alone in the house
- A collar and tag
- A leash
- A license
- A food bowl
- A water bowl
- Chew toys and other toys
- Dental biscuits
- Heartworm and flea medication
- Spay/neuter procedure (if not included in adoption fee or purchase price)
- First vaccinations (if not included in adoption fee or purchase price)
- Grooming supplies
- Poop scoop and waste disposal bags

These costs add up quickly, and a new dog can easily cost your family more than $1,000 when you have accumulated all of these things. Keep in mind that many of these essentials cost more for larger animals — a crate or leash for a 100-pound dog is probably going to be significantly more expensive than a crate or leash for a 10-pound dog. Dogs also take a chunk out of your monthly budget. You should expect to pay anywhere from $20 to $120 a month for food and grooming. Again, bigger dogs generally cost more than smaller ones, since they need more food and have more area to clean and brush. If you get a puppy or a young dog, you may also need to pay for obedience training classes or materials.

## Space

You do not have to have a lot of square footage to adopt a pet dog, but if you do not have much space, be sure you are comfortable with the idea of taking your dog out for a long walk every day. Having space to run and play is important to dogs, so if your indoor space does not accommodate that, you will need to get out and about at least once a day — even when the weather is nasty, you have a cold, or there is a big deadline at the office. It pays to do your research if your space is limited, since some types of dogs do better in small spaces while others may become destructive.

## Time

Dogs are one of the most time-consuming pets. Dogs generally need to be fed once or twice a day and given water to last them the day. They need at least one long exercise session each day, such as a walk or a trip to the dog park. They also need to be let out to use the bathroom three to six times a day.

A Dog's Life

There are more than 39 million pet dogs in the United States, according to the American Pet Products Manufacturing Association.

If you adopt a puppy or a dog that has not been trained, expect to spend even more time teaching your pet how to behave and housebreaking it. It is important to understand what dog training entails. *Learning how to train your dog is covered later in this chapter and in Chapter 9.* Even a well-trained dog may need you to spend more time with him or her early on as you establish house rules.

## Grooming

Grooming may sound like something that only happens to fancy show poodles when they get bows put in their hair, but all dogs need regular grooming to stay healthy.

**Bathing:** Expect to do this once a month or more if your dog needs it. You can do this by purchasing dog shampoo and using a tub outside or your bathtub, or you can have it done professionally at your vet's office or a professional groomer. (Though it is certainly less expensive to do your own grooming, you must be willing to get wet and deal with a sometimes-reluctant dog.)

**Brushing:** Your dog should be brushed at least once a week to prevent its hair from becoming tangled and matted, which can cause your dog discomfort. Your vet can recommend a brush you can buy and use at home, or you can have your dog's weekly brushing done by a professional groomer.

**Clipping claws:** Most dogs need claws clipped once a month, or whenever they get long. Not only is this important for your dog's overall hygiene, it also protects your furniture and can help to prevent unwanted scratches. You can ask your local pet store, the veterinarian, or have the vet show you how it is done, so that you can do it at home.

**Brushing teeth:** According to vets, your dog's teeth should be brushed at least once a week, with a dog toothbrush. (Ask your vet for a recommendation.) This helps prevent bad breath, something you will appreciate when your dog leaps up to give you a kiss.

Checking for fleas and ticks: If your pet spends time outside, it is imperative that you regularly check it for fleas and ticks. Ask your vet to show you what to look for if you are not sure how to spot fleas and ticks, but the easiest method is running a metal comb through your dog's coat, keeping it close to its skin. If black specs appear in the comb's teeth, that is flea dirt and is an indicator that your dog does have fleas. You can also ask for information about what you should do if you find a flea or tick on your dog.

## Well, Doggone!

Even if you think you know everything about dogs, these six facts may surprise you.

1. A dog's sweat glands are located between his paws.

2. A dog has 220,000,000 different smell receptors in its nose; that is more than four times what a human has.

3. A dog can learn to recognize as many as 1,200 different words, putting them intellectually on par with the average 2-year-old.

4. Forty percent of pet owners would choose a dog as their one companion on a desert island, according to a 2004 study by the American Animal Hospital Association.

5. Dogs can hear sounds that are as far as 250 yards away. Most people can only hear sounds within a 25-yard radius.

6. A dog's nose print is as unique as a person's fingerprint.

# Puppy vs. Dog

Once you are ready to commit to a dog, you must decide if you want to adopt or purchase a dog or puppy. There are advantages and challenges to either decision.

What is more adorable than a sweet, new puppy? However puppies require almost as great of a time investment as children do, and like your child, a puppy can sometimes drive you crazy with the sheer amount of work involved in keeping it healthy and happy.

It takes time for puppies to learn how to behave in a way that is conducive to a happy family life, and you should be prepared to deal with plenty of chewed-on furniture and stained floors in the process. Most puppies take about four months to properly house train; in the meantime, their owners must be vigilant to prevent and clean up accidents that inevitably occur. Keep in mind, too, that everything about your living environment — from enthusiastic yelling during a football game to the smell of chocolate chip cookies — is totally new to your puppy and will take time for it to get used to. Patience is key.

It is also important to remember that it is not safe to leave a young child alone with a puppy. Even the gentlest toddler can be too rough for a small puppy, and it is important that your child interact with your puppy only under supervision until you are totally confident that your child is mature enough to behave appropriately. Puppies are prone to nipping with their teeth and barking, either when they are afraid or when they are playing. This can be dangerous if you have small children, so this puppy tendency is worth keeping in mind as you make your decision.

Unlike puppies, adult dogs come with already-established personalities and behaviors. Most are already house trained, many have had obedience training, and a new dog is likely to need a few days — rather than a few weeks — to get used to your home and settle in as part of the family. By the time they exit the puppy stage, dogs have also started to exhibit their own personalities, so it is easier to tell if you are getting a calm or a playful dog. Plus, as dogs get older, they tend to calm down compared to an energetic puppy that always wants to play. Dogs are also sturdier than puppies and better know how to avoid your child's prodding fingers or feet without resorting immediately to biting. Ideally, you can adopt a dog who has lived with children or who has lots of experience with them.

## Housebreaking Your Dog

If you have decided to get a puppy that is not house trained, teaching your dog how to let you know when it has to go to the bathroom will be one of the first tasks you handle as a pet owner. If you have already gone through potty training at home, you will already be aware that patience and consistency are your best friends in the process of bathroom training. If you are still looking forward to your child's potty training days, consider housebreaking your new dog as good practice. Housebreaking your dog may take time and commitment, but it is not difficult. The Humane Society suggests several strategies to make house training go smoothly for you and your new pet:

**Start with a schedule:** Establish a routine so that your dog can depend on being fed, walked, and played with at the same times each day. Build your elimination breaks into your routine. If you have a puppy, the rule of thumb is one hour of elimination-safe time per month of age, so a 3-month-old puppy might be able to go three hours before needing a bathroom break. (An exception is bedtime, when most puppies can sleep for about seven hours without needing a potty break.)

**CReate oppoRtunities:** Take your dog outside frequently during the day, especially after he eats, drinks, or wakes up from a nap. The Humane Society says puppies do best with housebreaking when they go outside every two hours during the day. Praise your puppy enthusiastically when it eliminates outside to let it know that this is praiseworthy behavior. Praise it immediately after it goes rather than waiting until you are back home or inside, or it may not understand what the praise was for. Learn to recognize your pet's "I-gotta-go" cues — they usually take the form of barking, scratching, walking in circles, or sniffing the area around it — so that you can help it get outside quickly when it needs to make an elimination. If your puppy is inside and unsupervised, motivate it not to eliminate inside by keeping it in a small, enclosed area, like a crate — as long as you have properly crate trained your puppy.

**Be consistent:** Have a "bathroom spot" in your yard or park, and take your puppy there for every potty break so that it begins to associate that spot with using the bathroom. Create a routine that allows it to eliminate before beginning the rest of the walk or playtime so that it starts to understand that going to the bathroom is just part of the daily schedule.

**Be pRepaRed foR mishaps:** Much like toddlers, puppies are not going to be immediately housebroken. Your dog will probably have at least a few accidents on the road to successful house training. If you spot your puppy taking a bathroom break inside, make a loud noise to interrupt it and hustle it outside to its bathroom spot. If it finishes up outside, praise it and give your puppy a treat. If you find evidence of your puppy's bathroom break after the fact, clean the area thoroughly since your puppy will think it's OK to continue to use the bathroom in a spot that smells like the bathroom. Use a part water/part vinegar mixture to fully rid the spot of its smell. In either case, it is not recommended that you punish your puppy for the accident. Punishing your dog for accidents can actually make it more prone to having them, and if you try to punish after an accident has already taken place, your puppy probably will not understand what it is actually being punished for. Focus on rewarding good behavior rather than punishing accidents.

## What about crate training?

Crate training can be a good solution for families who want a pet dog but need a pet that can be confined for long stretches during the day. If you want to crate train your puppy, check with your vet, your local animal shelter, or a reputable pet store to get advice on humane crate training. Confining any animal to a small space has the potential to cause psychological harm to the animal if you do not do it properly, so while plenty of people crate train their dogs with absolutely no ill effects, you want to be sure that you are doing it the right way. Here are some general guidelines to follow if you decide to crate train your dog from the Humane Society of the United States:

1. Make the crate a comfortable spot for your dog. Settle it in an area where family members regular spend time so that

your dog's crate does not seem isolated, and add blankets or towels to make the crate comfortable.

2.  Let your dog explore its crate on its own by leaving the door open. Some dogs will be immediately drawn to the crate and may curl right up inside for a nap. Others may need encouragement in the form of favorite toys or snacks to venture inside the crate. Once your dog becomes comfortable with his crate, start serving his meals inside the crate.

3.  Start letting your dog stay in the crate for few minutes at a time. Always give your dog a treat and praise it for going into the crate, and stick close by the first few times you shut the door. Gradually, extend the length of time it stays in the crate and move to a different room for part or all of the time it is in the crate. Once your dog can handle being in the crate for 30 minutes with the family in another room, it is ready to stay crated for short periods of time while you are out of the house.

4.  Keep in mind that your dog should never stay in his crate for longer than three or four hours at a time, and it will need plenty of playtime and interaction during the rest of the day if it is spending time in his crate. Also, it is not a good idea to use your dog's crate as a punishment spot; this may cause it to develop negative associations for the crate. You want to make sure your dog's crate feels like a warm and welcoming place for your pet.

# Can Your Child Handle a Dog?

Before you decide to bring a dog into your family, make sure your child is ready to have a pet dog. If your child is not ready, it is better to wait a few months or years until he or she is prepared. Adopting a pet too soon may lead to an injured child or a pet that has to find a new home. Use the following guidelines to assess your child's readiness:

## Your child's age

There is no right age for dog ownership. The American Society for the Prevention of Cruelty to Animals suggests that parents should wait until a child is 6 years old to bring home a dog as a pet, but experts say a pet can be a fine addition to a family even with a newborn as long as the parents are willing to be responsible for taking charge of teaching their children about how to treat a dog. If you have a toddler, you will have to use a combination of teaching, vigilance and baby-proofing to keep your child from making a beeline for your new dog and pulling its tail and ears, the same way you would use those strategies to keep your child from sticking forks in the light socket or turning on the oven.

## Your child's health

Once you decide on a breed to adopt, make sure your child spends time with a similar dog to check for allergies and other reactions to the dog. If you are adopting a mutt, have your child spend time around a variety of dogs, including other mutts. Though it is not foolproof, doing pre-adoption testing can clue you in to whether allergies are likely to be a problem. (If your child is allergic and you have your heart set on a dog, do not worry: Different breeds cause different reactions, so trial and error is likely to point your family toward the right match for you.)

## Your child's play habits

Take a look at your child's toy shelf; are the toys still neat and whole, carefully played with and put away? Or are most of them broken and missing parts? If your child is rough with toys, he or she is likely to be rough with the family pet, so it is not a good idea to bring home a puppy or small dog. On the other hand, if your child is very careful and quiet, he or she may not take well to a very energetic dog that is always racing around knocking over the carefully built block towers. Keep your child's habits in mind as you try to decide which kind of dog is right for your new family pet.

## Your child's home habits

Does your child remember to do chores, or do you have to give lots of reminders? Does he or she forget homework at school and remember big projects at the last minute? Or is your child totally reliable and usually one step ahead of his or her to-do list? Your child's habits can show you his or her responsibility level, which can help you decide if you have the time and energy to devote to a young or high-maintenance dog, or if you have enough on your hands for now taking care of your child and would do better with a low-key dog who does not need a lot of maintenance or training. The more time you have to spend caring for your child, the less time you have to care for a pet. By the same token, as your child gets older, you should have more free time for a pet that needs a little more care.

## Your child's schedule

Kids today can have jam-packed schedules, and if your child has weeknight music lessons and weekends packed with homework, soccer practice, and community service work, a high-maintenance dog or one who needs lots of daily exercise may not be a good option. On the other hand, if your child spends a lot of time at home, he or she may be delighted to have a friendly dog to share his or her day with.

## Your child's experience with dogs

Before you bring home a dog, be sure to give your child the opportunity to spend time around dogs to see how he or she responds. Your child may be great playing rough and tumble with the neighbor's Labrador but terrify Grandmother's toy poodle with the same antics. Or you may realize that your daughter is overwhelmed by the vivacity of her cousin's energetic pet collie and enjoys spending time with calmer, quieter dogs that like cuddling more than careening. Observing your child's behavior with different kinds of dogs can be a valuable tool in deciding what kind of dog is the best fit for your child and your family.

# Finding the Right Dog

With more than 150 breeds of dogs and countless combinations available, finding the right dog can take time and effort — but it is absolutely worth it to find the pet that is right for your family. Here are some things to consider as you are looking at different dogs:

## Size

Dogs come in all sizes, and there are things to consider with larger and smaller dogs.

### Smaller dogs (Less than 18 pounds)

**Advantages:** Small dogs tend to live about four years longer than larger dogs. They also need less space, making them a good choice for families with limited living space or urban dwellings.

**But keep in mind:** Small dogs are more fragile than larger dogs and might be easily injured by an excited child. They may also be more likely to panic in a noisy or very active home and respond with biting and scratching.

### Medium-size dogs (Between 18 and 28 pounds)

**Advantages:** Medium-size dogs need less space than larger dogs and are usually sturdier than small dogs, so they can be a good option for families who do not have room for a big dog or who have small children that could hurt a small dog.

**But keep in mind:** Medium-size dogs still need space to run around and regular exercise.

### Larger dogs (more than 28 pounds)

**Advantages:** Sturdy, large dogs can handle the physical tumult of life with children and have plenty of energy to burn, making them a great choice for active households.

**But keep in mind:** Most larger dogs need plenty of space to run around or lots of regular exercise, so you need to make sure you have the space to accommodate that or the time to take the dog for long walks.

## Temperament

A dog's personality is the best indicator of how well it will fit into your family. Some aspects of a dog's personality are shaped by its breed — herder dogs like collies need lots of regular, challenging exercise to keep them sharp and happy — and some are formed through experiences. To check a potential dog's temperament:

- Sit with the dog in a quiet place and talk in a calm, friendly voice. If the dog tilts its head to one side or sits up more alertly, it is probably a responsive dog. If it takes it a few minutes of racing after its tail before calming down and pays attention to you, it probably has a lot of energy.

- To check how it responds to surprise noises, bring a rattle with you and shake it behind your back. If the dog perks up, looks curious, and starts searching for the source of the noise, it is probably going to handle unexpected household chaos with equal aplomb. If the dog reacts by barking, snarling, or biting, it might not do well in a busy household with children.

- Finally, check to see how the dog responds to being annoyed. Gently pull the dog's tail — but you do not want to hurt the dog — and see how it responds. If it makes it playful or if it pulls away from you without barking or biting, the dog has a reasonable pain tolerance and will likely have patience with children. If it snaps or bites at you, it might not be the right fit for a family.

## Top 10 Most-Likely-to-Bite Dogs

1. Chow
2. Shih Tzu
3. Lhasa apso
4. Toy terrier
5. Dachshund
6. Dalmatian
7. Chihuahua
8. Cocker Spaniel
9. Australian Cattle Dog
10. Akita

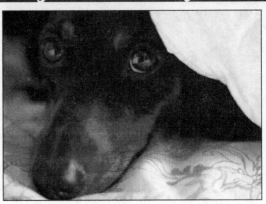

## Family-friendly Breeds

Once you have decided on a dog, it is time to choose what kind to get. Any dog can be good for a family, and there are exceptions to every rule; but in general, these breeds tend to do best with families.

### Labrador retrievers

**What makes them family-friendly:** Labs manage to combine the best qualities of a puppy — playful curiosity and a strong sense of fun — and the best qualities of a mature dog — patience with clumsy children and calm obedience even in chaos — for their entire lives. They are also incredibly adaptable dogs, which can do as well in city apartments as they do on country estates.

**What they need from you:** In addition to the basic dog care responsibilities listed earlier in this chapter, Labrador retrievers need more exercise than the average dog. They have a tendency to shed, so most need daily brushing, too.

## Golden retrievers

**What makes them family-friendly:**
Golden retrievers are always ready to play, making them a great addition to an active family. Cheerful, patient, and easy to train, golden retrievers have gorgeous coppery gold coats and an easy-going personality.

**What they need from you:** Because golden retrievers are playful and active, regular exercise that goes beyond daily walks is a must. Their pretty coats need regular brushing, too, to prevent tangles and matting.

## Boxers

**What makes them family-friendly:**
Muscular, sturdy boxers look like tiny guard dogs, but you would be hard-pressed to find a more playful pet. Boxers make incredibly loyal pets and forge strong bonds with their families. They are adventurous and curious, too, making them a good match for adventurous and curious kids.

**What they need from you:** Boxers need to burn off all that energy, so they do require lots of outdoor time each day, meaning they fit best with owners who can commit to daily brisk walks and playtime a few times a week or homes with big yards and plenty of room for running. They have short hair, but because they shed a lot, daily brushing is a good idea.

## Collies

**What makes them family-friendly:**
Lassie came by her maternal instincts naturally: Collies are herding dogs that are instinctively protective of and patient with children. Collies are also naturally good-spirited, unfailingly energetic, and surprisingly good mannered.

**What they need from you:** Collies need more exercise than the average dog, and just running around the block a few times will not cut it. They need creative play; so several weekly trips to the park to run obstacle courses and play fetch are a must. Collies are happiest when they are being challenged. Collies have a tendency to shed, so regular brushing (and a good vacuum cleaner) are essential.

## Yorkshire terriers

**What makes them family-friendly:**
If you are looking for a small dog, Yorkshire terriers might be the perfect choice. Unlike some other small dogs, Yorkshire terriers can handle households with children reasonably

well, though it is best to wait until your children are mature enough to understand what "be gentle" means if you want to get a small dog. Yorkshire terriers are little bundles of energy that get along with almost everyone and everything — including cats.

**What they need from you:** Because they are so small, Yorkies can get their exercise racing around a small apartment, making them ideal for families who live in the city or do not have an easily accessible outdoor space. Their long, silky fur needs daily brushing and regular shampooing.

## Miniature schnauzers

**What makes them family-friendly:** Miniature schnauzers have wiry coats of hair rather than fur, making them unlikely to cause allergies. They also do not shed, which can be a huge plus when it is cleaning time. In personality, miniature schnauzers are very vocal and affectionate. They also make good watchdogs.

**What they need from you:** Miniature schnauzers are happy to relax in the living room, so you can get away with skipping a night of exercise when it is rainy or cold. But be careful not to skip too much because it is easy for miniature schnauzers to gain weight if they do not get enough exercise.

## Getting Your Kids Involved

Though there is no question a dog is a family pet and you should never give any child sole responsibility for caring for an animal's welfare, there are plenty of ways your child can get involved in caring for your pet dog.

### Feeding

Feeding is one of the most important parts of caring for a pet, and children can get increasingly involved with this responsibility as they get older.

**Top 5 Dogs for Families with Allergies**

1. Soft Coated Wheaten Terrier
2. Basenji
3. Boston Terrier
4. Chinese Crested Hairless
5. Schnauzer (both Standard and Miniature)

**Toddlers and preschoolers** can help get the dog's food out at feeding time and help with washing and drying feeding bowls after a meal. They can also report when the water bowl needs refilling and help with filling it up.

**Elementary-school kids** can help with measuring out the proper amount of food, in addition to the chores listed previously.

**Older kids around 12 and up** can take over daily feeding chores — keep in mind that parents should monitor this to make sure the dog is being properly cared for — as well as helping with the chores mentioned previously.

## Grooming

Grooming is a daily or weekly responsibility, depending on the type of dog and its particular needs.

**Toddlers and preschoolers** can help by bringing the grooming kit or supplies to the grooming area and putting it away again after grooming. They can also sit quietly and calmly during grooming so that they can help keep the pet calm.

**Elementary-school kids** can help wash and dry paws after your dog's walk, in addition to the chores above. They can also help with brushing the dog.

**Older kids around 12 and up** can participate in grooming with adult supervision. They can help with the weekly check of your dog's teeth, eyes, and paws and with regular examinations for fleas and ticks, in addition to the previous responsibilities. They can also help with vacuuming and sweeping dog hair.

## Playing

Dogs need a lot of exercise to stay healthy, and children are a natural fit for these duties.

**Toddlers and preschoolers** can play with the dog and join the family on walks. They can help keep the dog's toys put away and make sure their own toys do not get mixed in with the dog's toys.

**Elementary-school kids** can tackle all the previous responsibilities, as well as helping fetch the dog's leash before walks and hanging it up again after the walk is over.

**Older kids around 12 and up** may be able to take the dog for walks on their own, in addition to the responsibilities listed above.

## CASE STUDY: DOING HIS DOGGY HOMEWORK

Parent: Linda Richland
Child: Jeremy
Atlanta, Georgia

Jeremy asked for a dog for every single birthday and Christmas from the time he was about 3 years old, but he and mom, Linda, live in an apartment in a fairly urban area, so Linda was not sure how they would handle a dog. Plus, she is a single mom and works full time. Jeremy goes to an after-school program and plays soccer three seasons, so Linda did not think a dog would really work with our life.

Jeremy was persistent, though. He spent a lot of time on the computer, researching information about how to care for a pet dog, and on his 12th birthday, he presented his mom with a detailed proposal. He had saved up $50, enough money to adopt a dog from our local shelter, and he showed her how he could save part of his allowance each week to pay for half of the dog food and supplies they needed. Jeremy explained that they needed a young dog rather than a puppy because they were not ready to handle something as involved as puppy training and house-breaking. He showed her research he had found about certain kinds of dogs who do well in smaller spaces. He thought a Yorkshire terrier or a Yorkie mix would do fine in their apartment, and he would be willing to take the dog for a walk every morning before breakfast. As for the evening walk, Jeremy reminded his mom that she kept talking about walking at night to get in shape, and a dog would give her the perfect motivation to do that.

Linda was impressed by how completely he had researched the topic. He had an answer for every question she asked him. When she was still unsure, he suggested that she could see how easy it would be for them to get a pet if she let him pet-sit for his friend Paul's mixed-breed dog while Paul was on vacation.

By the time Jeremy and Linda headed to their local shelter to check out a Yorkie mix that had been given up by its owners — Jeremy had gotten on the shelter's Yorkie wait list, more proof that he had done his doggy homework — Linda was confident that they were going to have a pet that would work well with their family. Sure enough, Yoda the Yorkie has been a great addition to their family.

# Chapter 4

Cats

## At a Glance

| | |
|---|---|
| **THE BEST PART**.................. | Cats are companionable, independent, and do well in indoor spaces of almost any size. |
| **THE BIGGEST CHALLENGE**..... | Cats can be a little too independent and do not always want to cuddle when their owners do. Owning a cat also means owning a litter box that has to be cleaned a few times a week. |
| **COST**............................. | Usually around $550 or more in start-up costs, including adoption or purchase, initial veterinarian visit, and starter gear, as well as approximately $20–$75 monthly for food and maintenance. |
| **NEEDS**............................ | Feeding once or twice daily, litter box cleaned daily or as needed, monthly grooming. |
| **AVERAGE LIFESPAN**............. | 15–17 years. |

Elegant, playful, and charming, cats are one of the most popular pets in the United States, beating out even dogs as family pets, according to the American Pet Products Manufacturing Association, who reports 64,250,000 pet cats in the United States as compared to 62,300,000 pet dogs. Though more families have pet dogs instead of cats, families who have pet cats are likely to have more than one cat.

A cat can be a delightful family pet. Since it does not need daily walks or regular bathroom breaks outside, a cat is not as high-maintenance as a dog and still has a high cuddle factor. This chapter will look at adopting a cat and the responsibilities it entails, highlighting some of the advantages and challenges of cat ownership, as well as considering which kinds of cats are best for families and how children can get involved in their pet's care.

## What Your Pet Cat Needs

Cats require less hands-on care than dogs, but they still need plenty of love and attention. Cats live for an average of 15–17 years, making them a long-term investment.

### Cost

Cat start-up costs can land someone around $550. Why so much? In addition to the adoption fee — which is usually between $25 and $100, but higher for some rescue organizations or specific breeds — or purchase price, you will need to invest in all the gear your new cat needs to be comfortable. This includes:

- A carrier for transport
- A food bowl

- A water bowl
- A litter box
- Litter and litter scoop
- A collar and tag
- Cat toys, scratching posts, and treats
- Heartworm and flea medication
- Spay/neuter procedure (if not included in adoption fee or purchase price)
- First vaccinations (if not included in adoption fee or purchase price)
- Grooming supplies

Cats also take a chunk out of their monthly budget. You can expect to spend around $20–$75 each month for food and litter in addition to the one-time, start-up costs.

## Space

Cats are comfortable in large or small spaces, but most experts recommend keeping pet cats exclusively as indoor pets. What is more important than the size of your space is making sure that you have a private, secure, and accessible place to store your cat's litter box as well as her food. You will want to be sure that your cat's food and litter are not too near each other and that both are easy for your cat to get to, but difficult for young children to get into. A baby gate can protect your cat's area, or consider putting your cat's gear on a shelf in a laundry room or other quiet place.

## Time

While cats need significantly less hands-on time than dogs, it is important that you have plenty of time to spend at home with your pet. Though they are independent, cats are very social creatures and like playing and spending time with their family. If you adopt a kitten or a cat that has not been socially trained or house trained, you should expect to invest a significant amount of time early on in training your new pet in using its litter box and following the house rules.

## Grooming

Cats are famously fastidious, and you will frequently see your cat cleaning itself. In fact, it does not need a lot of help from you to stay clean, but there are a few things it does need help with now and again.

**Bathing**: If you brush your cat's fur regularly, it will seldom need a bath — cats are naturally clean. But if your cat has gotten into something particularly smelly or dirty or if its coat is greasy or matted, a bath is a good idea. You can bathe it at home in the kitchen sink with a few extra hands or take it to a professional groomer for bathing.

**Brushing**: Short-haired cats generally need brushing once a week; long-haired cats do better with daily brushing. Brushing spreads your cat's natural oils through its fur, keeping it in healthy condition and removing dirt and irritants. A groomer can do this if you would rather not, but it is usually easier and less expensive to brush your cat yourself, since for most cats it requires no special skill. If you are slightly allergic to cat hair or if your cat is very sensitive to grooming, you might consider hiring a professional to help you.

**Clipping:** Clipping is one of the most important tasks of a cat owner because long claws are dangerous for your family and uncomfortable for the cat — not to mention a hazard for the furniture. Most cats need clipping once a month, but some cats need their claws clipped more frequently. You can purchase a clipper and do it yourself or take your pet to a groomer or veterinarian to have its claws clipped. If you decide to take on the task of clipping yourself, ask a vet or groomer to demonstrate the process for you. You should trim just the claw and not the quick, or you could cause pain and bleeding for your cat.

## What about declawing?

Many people — especially those with young children or expensive furniture — consider declawing cats to keep those pesky and dangerous claws from causing any damage. This process, which surgically removes the first knuckle of each of the cat's toes, is both painful and dangerous and should be avoided at all costs. It often backfires, too: Declawed cats may be more likely to bite or spray than cats who have their natural defense mechanism available to them.

If your cat is prone to scratching, and you are worried about protecting your child or your new couch, declawing your cat can be a tempting option. If you are considering declawing, look into other alternatives, such as Soft Paws® claw covers (**www.soft-paws.com**) that sheath dangerous claws in vinyl caps or having a professional trainer work with your cat to use a scratching post. Many veterinarians are hesitant to do onychectomy — the technical name for the surgery that removes a cat's claws — unless you have unsuccessfully tried other methods of managing your cat's scratching habits. The American Veterinary Medical Association supports the procedure only in extreme cases.

If you do decide to declaw your cat, talk to your veterinarian about possible risks and side effects for your pet. Be aware that declawed cats are extremely vulnerable and must be kept indoors.

## Kitten vs. Cat

Once you are ready to commit to a cat, you must decide if you want to adopt a cat or a new kitten. There are advantages and challenges to either decision.

Everybody loves a kitten: Little more than a meowing ball of fluff, kittens are utterly enchanting. They are also a lot like toddlers in that they require a lot of patience and almost constant supervision. If you choose to adopt a kitten, you will need to be prepared to teach it how to behave, including how to use the litter box, and you will need to be prepared for some scratched furniture and fingers in the process.

Kittens are also small and fragile, so it is easy for eager children to hurt them without meaning to do so. At the same time, it is easy for them to hurt you or your child in their excitement since they have not really learned how not to bite and scratch. Kittens are also a bit difficult to read. You can look for behavior clues, but in the end your cat's personality will develop as it grows up with you, and the personality it develops may or may not mesh well with your household. Of course, a pet that grows up with your family may adapt better to life in your family.

On the other hand, older cats have established personalities, so it is easier to tell if they are already comfortable around children. If you are looking for a playful cat or hoping to find one that is very calm, it is easy to do when the cat in question already has a his or her history of behavior. You can even look specifically for a cat that has previously lived with children and is used to a family home. Adopting a cat also means you will spend less time on training and helping your new pet adapt. A cat will likely need a few days to adjust to its new home, while a kitten might need a few months to comfortably settle in.

## Feline Facts

Think you know everything there is to know about cats? These facts may surprise you.

1. A litter of kittens is called a kindle.

2. Most cats sleep for 16 hours every day.

3. Sir Isaac Newton, who is credited with the discovery of the principles of gravity as well as other significant scientific breakthroughs, also invented the cat door in the early 18th century.

4. The average house cat spends about 10,950 hours of its life purring.

5. A cat's heart beats between 110 and 140 times a minute, about twice the speed of a person's heart.

6. Cats spend about 30 percent of their waking time each day grooming.

# Pick of the Litter Box

Cats may need a little help to get the hang of using a litter box, but because they are such fastidious creatures, they tend take to it fairly easily. One thing you will want to keep in mind is that cats can tolerate very different levels of litter box maintenance: Some cats may act out by urinating on your bed if you do not change the litter box twice a day while others are fine with their litter boxes being changed just once a week. In general, a quick daily scoop is ideal, but you should match your routine to your cat's needs. (You will pick up on your cat's routine after only a few days.)

Introduce your cat to your litter box when you show it the rest of your home, and gently scratch its paws in the litter. This movement — the same one it uses to cover waste — clues that this is its potty place. If your cat has an accident, use a paper cloth to wipe up the mess, then put it into her litter box. Gently put your cat in the litter box and again scratch its claws in the litter. You may have to do this a few times before your cat masters using the litter box.

Do not punish your cat when it has accidents. Remember, it is still learning. Instead, use accidents as an opportunity to reinforce the idea that the litter box is the place to eliminate waste, and praise your cat when it gets it right.

## Make your own nontoxic kitty litter

Eco-friendly products are beneficial to the environment and to your family, especially when you have young children in the house. Your kids can help you make your own non-toxic litter for your pet cat with this environmentally friendly recipe.

1.  Shred one entire newspaper into strips and wash it in soapy water, using sink detergent.

2.  Stir newspaper strips and soapy water until it is the consistency of oatmeal.

3.  Take newspaper concoction and place it in a colander.

4.  Rinse with clear warm tap water.

5.  Add enough baking soda to newspaper to soak up any moisture.

6.  Wearing rubber gloves, knead the substance like bread dough, squeezing out excess moisture. The substance will start to dry and break up.

7.  Break the substance into small pebble-sized pieces. Crumble until it is all in small bits.

8.  Lay it out on a screen to dry. It may take several days until it is completely dry.

9.  When it is dry, put about 2 inches of the paper crumbles in the litter box, scoop out solids daily, and change it once a week.

## Can Your Child Handle a Cat?

Before you decide to bring a cat into your family, make sure your child is ready to have a pet cat. It is better to wait a few months or years than to bring home a cat and have it or your child end up injured or returning the cat to a shelter. Consider your child's behaviors using the following guidelines:

## Your child's age

Most experts recommend that families with children younger than 6 forego getting a kitten and favor getting a cat that is at least 2 years old. Cats are relatively small creatures and can easily be hurt by curious children, so if you have a toddler, you will need to be ready to baby-proof, teach, and be on your guard to be sure your child does not damage his or her new pet. Because cats are fairly independent, they can be a good fit for houses with toddlers or young children who need a lot of attention themselves.

## Your child's health

Once you decide on a breed to adopt, make sure your child spends time with a similar cat to check for allergies and other reactions to the cat. If you are adopting a mixed breed cat — usually described as an American short-hair cat or an American long-hair cat — have your child spend time around other mixed breed cats. Though it is not fail-proof, doing pre-adoption testing can clue you in to whether allergies are likely to be a problem. If your child is allergic and you have your heart set on a cat, do not worry: Different breeds cause different reactions, so trial and error is likely to point your family toward the right match for you.

## Your child's play habits

Does your child play well with other children, or does he or she get a little rough? Is your child respectful or playground rules, or do you have to regularly remind him or her to wait his turn or not push other children? If your child has trouble remembering to be careful with his or her friends, he or she is likely to be rough with the family pet, so it is not a good idea to bring home a kitten or very small or delicate cat. A child can kill a kitten just by stepping on it accidentally. On the other hand, if your child is very careful and quiet, he or she may not take well to very energetic cat that is constantly batting at his or her book when he or she is trying to read. Keep your child's habits in mind as you try to decide which kind of cat is right for your new family pet.

## Your child's home habits

Does your child leave the water running when her or she brushes her teeth and constantly forget to turn off lights when he or she leaves a room? Or can you count on her to have her teeth brushed every morning without a reminder? Your child's habits can show you how responsible he or she is, which can help you decide if you have the time and energy to devote to a young or high-maintenance cat, or if you already have enough training on your hands for now and would do better with a low-key cat who does not need a lot of maintenance or training.

## Your child's schedule

Kids today can have busy schedules, and if your child has weeknight music lessons and weekend packed with homework, soccer practice and community service work, a high-maintenance cat may not be an option. If your child spends a lot of time at home, a cat might be a good companion.

## Your child's experience with cats

Before you bring home a cat, be sure to give your child the opportunity to spend time around cats to see how he or she responds. Your child may have a enjoy a playful cat but get his or her feelings hurt by the dismissive avoidance of the neighbor's less-exuberant cat. Observing your child's behavior with different kinds of cats can be a valuable tool in deciding what kind of cat is the best fit for your child and your family.

# Finding the Right Cat

Choosing the right cat for your family means considering the pros and cons of various cats. Here are some factors to weigh in your considerations.

## Coat

When it comes to coats, cats can have short, thick fur or long, fluffy fur. Which one you choose is really based on your preference.

### Short hair

**Advantages:** Short-haired cats need less grooming since it is harder for their coats to get tangled.

**But keep in mind:** Short-haired does not mean they shed less: some short-haired cats shed more than their long-haired friends.

### Long hair

**Advantages:** Long-haired cats' silky coats make them super soft.

**But keep in mind:** Long hair tangles easily, and a long-haired cat will need more grooming than a short-haired cat.

## Temperament

A cat's personality is the best indicator of how well it will fit into your family. The breed shapes some aspects of a cat's personality and some are formed through its experiences. To check a potential cat's temperament:

- Sit with it in a quiet place and talk in a calm, friendly voice. If the cat approaches you and butts its head affectionately against your hand or legs, it is probably a responsive cat.

- To check how a cat responds to surprise noises, bring a rattle with you and shake it behind your back. If it responds by hissing and scratching, this cat might not do well in a busy household with children.

- Finally, check to see how the cat responds to being annoyed. Gently pull the cat's tail or stroke its soft, sensitive belly — you do not want to hurt the cat — and see how it responds. If the cat pulls away from you without hissing, scratching, or biting or tolerates you touching its underside, it has a reasonable pain tolerance and will likely have patience with children. If it scratches or bites, it might not be the right fit for a family.

## Family-friendly Breeds

While mixed-breed cats are most common, some pedigreed cats are becoming popular again through breeders and rescue groups, and some are known for their family-friendly characteristics.

### Persian

**What makes them family-friendly:** Inaddition to being adorable — with long, silky fur and sweet, flat faces — Persians are about as cuddly and affectionate as it is possible for a cat to be. They will snuggle in your child's lap for an entire movie, purring the whole time.

**What they need from you:** Because they give a lot of love, Persians need a lot of love in return, so be prepared for lots of petting and cuddle time. Their long fur also needs daily brushing to prevent snarls and tangles.

## American Shorthair

**What makes them family-friendly:**

American Shorthair cats are sturdy, playful, and full of intelligence and curiosity, making them an ideal companion for growing children. They can keep going as long as your kids can, which is not always easy to do. American Shorthair cats are also laid back and even-tempered, and get along well with children and other pets.

**What they need from you:** Because American Shorthair cats may be prone to obesity, working with your veterinarian to choose the right food for your cat is very important. American Shorthair cats have thick, short fur, which needs weekly grooming. These cats are very playful, so it is important to have make time in your schedule for playtime.

## Abyssinian

**What makes them family-friendly:**

Abyssinians are the original domesticated cats — descendants from the feline companions of the ancient Egyptians — and the intelligence, curiosity, and playfulness that made them such a hit with the ancient Egyptians are likely to make them a hit with active families, too.

**What they need from you**: Because Abyssinians are so active, they need owners who have plenty of time to play with them. Also, because they are purebreds, Abyssinians need to be kept inside as much as possible to prevent contagious diseases that may be carried by stray cats and other animals. They also need weekly grooming.

## Maine Coon

**What makes them family-friendly**: Hardy Maine Coon cats are too busy playing to have much time to sit and cuddle, which makes them a great fit for active families. These sturdy cats — many of which have distinctive, raccoon-like ringed tails — love to chase and can even be taught to play fetch.

**What they need from you**: As with any active pet, Maine Coon cats need plenty of exercise and playtime every day. Most have easy-to-care-for coats that require only weekly grooming. Unlike many cats that avoid contact with water, Maine Coons love splashing in their water bowls with their paws; so it is important to make regular checks to ensure their water bowls are clean and full of fresh water.

# Getting Your Kids Involved

As with dogs, cats should not have to rely on a child for their care. But even if your child does not take full responsibility for a pet cat, there are plenty of ways he or she can get involved in caring for a cat.

## Feeding

Feeding is one of the most important parts of caring for a pet, and children can get more involved with this responsibility as they get older. Cats generally need to be fed once a day, and you can leave their bowl out so they can eat whenever they want to during the day and night.

**Toddlers and preschoolers** can help get out the cat's food at feeding time and help with washing and drying feeding bowls as needed. They can also report when the water bowl needs refilling and can even help fill it up.

**Elementary-school kids** can help with measuring out the proper amount of food, in addition to the chores listed previously.

**Older kids around 12 and up** can take over daily feeding chores — keep in mind that parents should monitor this to make sure the cat is being properly cared for — as well as helping with the chores mentioned previously.

## Grooming

Grooming is a daily or weekly responsibility, depending on the type of cat your family has and its particular needs.

**Toddlers and preschoolers** can help by bringing the grooming kit or supplies to the grooming area and putting it away again after grooming. They can also sit quietly and calmly during grooming to help your cat stay calm.

**Elementary-school kids** can help with your cat's regular brushing, in addition to the chores above.

**Older kids around 12 and up** can participate in grooming with adult supervision. They can help with the weekly check of your cat's teeth, eyes, and paws and with regular examinations for fleas and ticks, in addition to the previous responsibilities. They can also help with vacuuming and sweeping cat hair and with some litter box duties, including holding the bag for parents as you remove litter and helping to disinfect the litter box between cleaning.

## Playing

Playing is a necessary part of life for a healthy cat, and it is often a child's favorite part of cat care.

**Toddlers and preschoolers** can pet and play with a cat with adult supervision. They can also give cats treats with adult supervision.

**Elementary-school kids** can begin to learn how to play with a cat using its toys, teaching it to jump and run and rewarding it with treats.

**Older kids around 12 and up** who have shown themselves to be responsible and mature with their pet can play with it unsupervised, though frequent parental checks are always a good idea. They can also participate in the above-mentioned care duties.

## CASE STUDY: KITTY IN PERIL

Parent: Maggie Hutchinson
Child: Lily
Abilene, Texas

*The Hutchinson family has two cats, Night and Day. Lily named them. She was 4 years old when they got the cats from an animal shelter, and she thought the yellow-striped cat looked like daytime, while the black cat with one white ear looked like night.*

From the beginning, Lily has been crazy about the family's pets. Sometimes when she was little, she would get too excited, and Maggie would have to remind her to be careful. They had a code: If Maggie said, "Oh, no, kitty in peril," it meant that Lily had to calm down and leave the cats alone for a few minutes. (To this day, they still say "Kitty in peril" sometimes.) Lily really liked to hold the cats and could not understand why they did not always want her to be holding them. There were definitely a few scratches early on as Lily and the cats learned how to deal with each other.

Now that Lily is 9 years old, she shares a lot of responsibilities for pet care. She makes sure that Night and Day have fresh food every day and adds fresh litter to their litter box a couple of times a week. (Maggie handles the water because Lily still has trouble carrying the bowls without spilling, and isn't great at cleaning out the old litter.) She spends about an hour a day playing with her pets — Night will play fetch with her and bring back small toys Lily throws at him while Day likes to chase feathers on a string that Lily pulls through the air. She usually plays with them after dinner when she is watching television. Sometimes Night will curl up on Lily's stomach while she is reading. (Day does not like to cuddle, but she will perch on a nearby windowsill to watch.)

Maggie definitely thinks owning a pet has made Lily more responsible than other 9-year-olds. She really understands what it takes to care for a living creature, and Maggie is proud of how responsible her daughter is and how gentle she has become with her pets.

# Chapter 5

Birds

## At a Glance

**THE BEST PART**.................  Birds are beautiful and interesting pets who can largely fend for themselves. Many birds make pleasant noises and will enjoy "talking" to your child.

**THE BIGGEST CHALLENGE**.....  Birds can make a big mess, so expect to clean up the cage at least once a week with a few smaller cleanings throughout the week. Because birds are not naturally domesticated the way most domestic dogs and cats are, each of them needs to be individually trained.

**COST**..........................  Usually around $700 or more in start-up costs, including adoption or purchase, initial veterinarian visit, and starter gear and about $20 a month for food and maintenance.

**NEEDS**............................ Pet birds need to have their cages cleaned weekly. They need daily food and water and to have their food and water containers cleaned each day. They also need regular grooming — the frequency of this grooming depends on the type of bird — of wings, nails, and beak.

**AVERAGE LIFESPAN**............. 10–60 years.

Birds are the third most common type of pet in the United States, coming just after dogs and cats in popularity. Birds can be a welcome addition to a family home, according to Vera Appleyard, who runs the Parrot Parrot Web site (**www.parrotparrot.com**), a site devoted to the care and keeping of parrots, because birds are flock animals and see themselves as part of the "family flock." They thrive in homes with children, where they can add their voices to the general bustle of family life. As with any pet, there are challenges and advantages to making a bird part of your family. Here are some things to keep in mind as you are choosing your new pet if you have decided that a bird is the right fit for your family.

## What Your Pet Bird Needs

Depending on your lifestyle, a bird can be the ultimate low-maintenance or high-maintenance pet. On one hand, they can be fairly expensive to acquire, with relatively high purchase costs and a lot of necessary paraphernalia; on the other hand, their monthly needs are relatively modest. They are low-maintenance pets that do not need the extensive daily playtime like dogs and cats do and are largely happy to fend for themselves; but adopting a bird means making numerous household accommodations, including getting rid of a number of common household items.

## Cost

Expect to pay around $700 in start-up costs for your bird. Why so much? In addition to the adoption fee or purchase price (which can range from $10 (for a small bird such as a parakeet) to more than $5,000 (for certain types of large parrots and cockatoos) and varies greatly among specific breeds, you will need to invest in all the gear your new bird needs to be comfortable. This includes:

- A cage large enough for your bird to fully extend its wings and fly a short distance
- Perches
- Feeding bowl
- Water tube
- Cage liners
- Cage cleaning solution and supplies
- Bathing dishes
- Toys and treats
- Initial vet visit (to an avian veterinarian who has bird-specific experience)
- Grooming supplies

Birds also take a chunk out of the monthly budget. You can expect to spend around $20 each month for food and other supplies, in addition to the one-time, start-up costs.

## Space

If you provide them a large enough cage and let your bird out for supervised inside flights during the day, a bird can be as happy in a tiny city apartment as in a sprawling country house. More important than the square footage of your home is what is inside it. A number of common household items can be dangerous and even toxic for birds, including:

- **Teflon® or nonstick cookware:** When heated, these pans give off an odorless fume that is fatal to birds in just minutes so you will need to change the way you cook if you have a pet bird.

- **Scented candles and air fresheners:** These products can pose a hazard to bird's sensitive respiratory system.

- **Cigarettes:** Smoking is potentially hazardous for birds, which means if you have not kicked the habit, you will have to take smoke breaks outside and wash your hands thoroughly after smoking before handling your bird.

- **Houseplants:** Believe it or not, many common houseplants are toxic to birds, so you will need to check with an experienced avian veterinarian about what is hazardous to your particular bird. (As always, "when in doubt, throw it out" is a good rule of thumb when it comes to your pet bird's safety.)

- **Avocado, chocolate, and coffee beans:** These foods can be toxic for your pet bird if ingested. You do not have to get rid of them, but you should store them securely in a place your pet cannot access.

- **Insecticides:** These can be harmful or fatal to your pet.

You will also want to scour your space (and possibly your family's wardrobe) for shiny objects that your bird will be attracted to and to keep them out of your bird's line of vision to protect your objects or jewelry and your pet from potential harm.

## Time

The biggest time cost of having a bird is maintaining cleanliness. Birds make plenty of mess in and around their cages, so expect to have a busy cleaning schedule.

### Daily

- Replace the cage's paper liners
- Wash and thoroughly dry food containers and water dishes
- Clean birdbath
- Clean any toys or perches
- Sweet or vacuum the area around the cage

### Weekly

- Remove all gear from cage and clean thoroughly inside and out
- Clean all toys and gear and disinfect them
- Clean and disinfect the cage apron
- Clean and disinfect the floor under the cage
- Clean and disinfect the walls around the cage (Ask your pet store to recommend a bird-friendly disinfectant, such as Mango Pet Focus Avian Bird Cage Cleaner)

Birds also need daily exercise, which can be as simple as letting them out of their cages for a short time to fly around a closed-off room that has been bird-proofed. It is important to interact with your bird every day, since birds are not naturally domesticated creatures and even trained birds require daily handling and interaction to maintain their domesticated ways.

## Grooming

Keeping your bird clean and healthy is an important part of bird ownership. Here is what you can expect when it comes to grooming a pet bird.

**Bathing**: Birds will clean themselves, but they rely on their owners to provide them with the tools to do it. One of the simplest solutions is to set out bathing dishes, shallow containers of room temperature water, several times each week. If you would prefer to skip the birdbaths, some birds can be gently misted with warm water once or twice a week. In either case, it is important for birds to have perches for preening and grooming themselves with their beaks immediately after baths.

**Trimming nails**: Your bird's nails will need regular trimming — how often depends on the type of bird, but generally if the nails are long enough to keep the bird's foot from sitting flat on the floor or if the nails are dangerously sharp, it is time for a trim. You can do this yourself or have an avian grooming professional or veterinarian do it for you. If you plan to do it yourself, it is smart to watch someone else perform the trimming before you try it so that you can get a sense of how long the nails should be and how to keep your bird comfortable during the process.

**Trimming beaks**: If your bird's beak appears to be wearing down unevenly, your avian veterinarian should see him or her to determine why and to trim the beak to prevent possible difficulties with eating and preening. You should not attempt to trim your bird's beak yourself because if it is done incorrectly, you could permanently injure your pet.

**Clipping Wings:** For birds allowed out of their cages at all, clipping wings is an important part of protecting your pet's safety. Birds with unclipped wings can smash into windows, dive into pots of boiling water, or fly into ceiling fans, so although clipping may seem cruel, it is imperative if you are going to keep a bird as a pet. Clipping the new growth on the outer wings helps keep birds from flying too high and getting hurt. You can trim them yourself, but it is smart to have an avian veterinarian do it the first few times it is needed so that you can learn how to clip your bird's wings properly. A mistake in clipping can interfere with your bird's ability to fly straight and even cause damage and bleeding. Birds' wings grow like fingernails, so expect to trim them periodically.

## Can Your Child Handle a Bird?

Birds are sensitive, fragile animals, even more so than small dogs and cats. Too-harsh handling easily injures their tiny, hollow bones, and their delicate wings can be damaged by too-rough play. Plus, birds use their beaks much the same way they use their claws — to achieve leverage and to aid in climbing — so even friendly birds sometimes bite, so you should be sure your child knows what and what not to do. Consider these factors when deciding whether a bird is right for your family.

## Your child's age

Because birds are much more fragile than cats and dogs, most experts recommend not even considering a bird as a pet until children are at least 6 years old and have proven they are able to control their impulses and act responsibly. Birds tend to bond with the people who take care of them and interact with them, so if your child is not old enough to help with some of the bird care responsibilities, he or she may be disappointed to find that your family pet is not very affectionate toward him or her. For these reasons, it is usually smart to wait until your child is old enough to be a responsible bird owner to bring one home, even if it means waiting a little longer than you had originally hoped.

## Your child's health

Allergies to birds result mainly from feather dander. Since each breed of bird has a unique dander, it is important to be sure that your child spends time around a bird of the breed you are con-sidering to check for possible allergies. Get in touch with a local bird society to see if a member with the type of bird you are con-sidering would be open to letting your child visit his or her pet. It is also important to keep the area around your bird's cage clean since the area can quickly become unhygienic for your child and your pet without regular cleaning.

## Your child's play habits

Is your child patient with complicated puzzles and projects that require extra time and careful handling, or does he or she get frustrated and fling his or her toys on the floor? If your child is not careful with his or her toys, he or she is likely to be rough with the family pet, so a delicate bird might not be a good fit for your child right now. If you have your heart set on a pet bird, it would be wise to wait until your child is more mature and careful.

## Your child's home habits

Does your child wreak havoc on rooms during playtime, or is he or she quick to tidy up messes as they appear? Your child's habits can show you how responsible she is. Because birds are especially fragile, it is important that your child prove herself to be responsible and mature before you bring one home as a pet.

## Your child's schedule

Most birds do fine with plenty of quiet time, so a busy schedule is not a deterrent to getting a pet bird. Just be sure your child is not away from the house significantly more than the rest of the family, or he or she may miss out on the opportunity to bond with the family pet. Birds need daily care, but they do not mind spending chunks of time on their own.

## Your child's experience with birds

Before you bring home a bird, be sure to give your child the opportunity to spend time around birds to see how he or she responds. He or she may sing happily along with the neighbor's songbirds or start sobbing hysterically if frightened by an outspoken parrot. Observing your child's behavior with different kinds of birds can be a valuable tool in deciding what kind of bird is the best fit for your child and your family.

# BiRd BRains

Interested in owning a pet bird? Show off your avian savvy with one of these unusual facts about our feathered friends.

1. Birds do not sweat. Instead, they rely on the air they breathe to help them cool off. As much as 75 percent of a bird's oxygen intake goes to regulating its temperature.

2. A bird's heart beats up to 1,000 times a minute when it is flying. It is still fast when a bird is resting — about 400 beats a minute.

3. A bird's feathers weigh more than its entire skeleton does.

4. Birds have a keen sense of hearing, but they do not have external ears.

5. Birds are probably the most direct descendants of dinosaurs alive today.

## Finding the Right Bird

Choosing the right bird for your family requires you to consider which qualities are the best fit for your family's life. Listed below are some of the factors you might want to weigh as you are making your decision.

### Size

Birds come in a variety of sizes, and whatever size you choose comes with a variety of benefits and challenges.

### Small birds (12 inches or smaller)

**Advantages:** Small birds — such as budgies and cockatiels — take up minimal house space. Since birds need plenty of room to move around inside their cages, it is much easier to comfortably house a smaller bird in limited space.

**But keep in mind:** Small birds are particularly fragile; in addition to being potentially menaced by clumsy children, they may be easy to accidentally sit or step on when out of their cage.

## Large birds (Larger than 12 inches)

**Advantages:** Sturdier large birds are usually good with children and will be able to handle more direct contact than smaller birds.

**But keep in mind:** Larger birds also mean larger beaks, and since biting is almost inevitable with pet birds, bigger beaks can translate to more painful bites. (A nip from a smaller bird might cause a sharp pain, but a chomp from a larger bird could do serious damage to your whole finger.) Larger birds also need more space and — if their quarters are on the cramped side — more daily flying time outside the cage.

## Sociability

Some birds prefer to spend time alone in their cages; others cannot get enough family time. Think carefully about which sort of bird best fits your family's needs. Some birds, such as cockatoos, enjoy being held and even cuddled, while other birds will avoid you when you try to hold them. What kind of bird do you prefer? Would you like an affectionate, playful bird, or are you more interested in a bird that is content to be left alone most of the time?

## Noise

Birds can be quite loud, and keep in mind that birds in homes with children are generally even louder. Because birds have a natural flock mentality, when your children get loud, your pet bird is likely to join in. This tendency toward increased loudness is something to keep in mind if your children have already reached the top of your sound threshold. If you live in an apartment or condominium, keep in mind that loud noises have the potential to disturb your neighbors and may violate your homeowners' association bylaws. Some birds have beautiful singing voices. Others can learn to

**Good Morning, Sunshine**

Birds are early risers, which means most birds will loudly demand their breakfast bright and early, even on a sleepy Saturday morning. For parents with young children who are used to early morning wake-up calls, this might not be an issue, but remember that your bird will still be waking up with the sun even when your little one is finally willing to sleep later than 7 a.m. If you are looking forward to sleeping in again, a bird might not be the right pet for your family.

talk and repeat words and phrases, which many children find delightful. Still others are quieter and seldom vocalize at all. Your preferences should dictate which bird is the best fit for your particular family.

## Family-friendly Birds

There are hundreds of different types of birds, but the breeds listed below are usually good with children and therefore tend to make good family pets. Budgies and cockatiels are respectively the first and second most common pet birds in families with children.

## Budgies

### What makes them family-friendly:

Budgies, also called parakeets, are calm, quiet birds with gorgeously vivid feathers and sweet personalities. Unlike most birds, they are also fairly neat and less prone to making a mess. They can sometimes be taught to speak, but most are content to whistle. They love attention and are very playful.

### What they need from you:
Budgies need lots of love and attention and respond well to conversation, petting, and play time. Budgies are curious, intelligent birds that need lots of toys and activity to stay happy. Because budgies are very active, most need their wings clipped for safety reasons; all need their nails to be clipped regularly.

## Cockatiels

### What makes them family-friendly:

With their distinctive, lovely appearance and soft voices, cockatiels make a charming family pet. They can be taught to mimic voices, but their real talent is whistling, and your pet cockatiel can delight your family with spot-on renditions of favorite tunes if you give your bird a chance to learn them. Cockatiels are sweet natured and usually very affectionate.

**What they need from you**: Cockatiels need plenty of room in their cages to fly around, including at least two perches to hop or fly between and plenty of toys to keep them busy. Cockatiels thrive on attention and do best when their cage is centrally located and near the hub of daily activity. They need twice-weekly baths to stay well groomed and keep their feathers healthy. Cockatiels need regular nail clipping; most should have their wings clipped.

## Canaries

**What makes them family-friendly:** Their beautiful singing voices make canaries a delight to have around the house. Since they prefer minimal physical contact and do not need very much space, they can be a good option for a family who has young children or who would prefer a "look-but-do not-touch" pet that can be kept safely out of the children's reach.

**What they need from you**: Canaries love baths and should be given the opportunity to bathe at least twice weekly; setting out baths in their cage will do the trick. Their nails need to be clipped regularly.

## African Grays

**What makes them family-friendly:**
These softly hued gray parrots have been called the best talkers of all parrots and can mimic sounds such as ringing telephones and car horns as well as human voices. They are playful and generally good-natured and prefer a healthy dose of alone time to balance with their companionship.

**What they need from you:** African Grays do best with regular baths, but wing clipping should be kept to a minimum since clipped wings can exacerbate African Grays' natural tendency to fall. African Grays also need plenty of toys — including chew toys — or they are likely to become bored and rambunctious.

# Getting Your Kids Involved

Your child should never have sole responsibility for caring for a pet bird, but there are a number of ways your child can participate in caring for your family pet.

## Feeding

Feeding is one of the most important parts of caring for a pet, and children can get increasingly involved with this responsibility as they get older.

**Toddlers and preschoolers** can help with checking the bird's dish for any wetness before it is filled up — this is an important job since wetness can cause bird food to mold quickly.

**Elementary-school kids** can, in addition to the job above, help measure out the correct amount of food for your pet bird, as well as helping to wash and dry feeding dishes.

**Older kids around 12 and up** can do all of the above, as well as helping with cleaning the cage and the area around it after feeding time and with the weekly disinfecting duties.

## Grooming

Different grooming tasks need to be done daily and weekly, depending upon on the type of bird your family has and its particular needs.

**Toddlers and preschoolers** can help fill birdbaths or shallow dishes for your bird to use to clean itself.

**Elementary-school kids** can learn how to gently mist your pet bird with warm water to help it clean itself. They can also fetch grooming supplies when it is nail-clipping time in addition to the above responsibilities.

**Older kids around 12 and up** can do everything younger kids can do, plus measure out and supply bird food and fresh water and check your bird's water supply throughout the day.

## Playing

Playing with your pet is one of the most enjoyable parts of pet ownership for kids. With birds, playtime is especially important since birds bond with their caretakers and may be antisocial with people they do not perceive as their caretakers. If you have a pet bird, be sure your child participates in playtime with it on a regular basis, even if you are not comfortable with your child assuming the other care-taking responsibilities described in this section. Keep in mind: Some birds are more social than others and enjoy playtime, while others would rather be left alone.

**Toddlers and preschoolers** can talk to and sing with a pet bird.

**Elementary-school kids** can also do that, plus learn how to carefully hold their pet bird on a finger and play with it with its toys, with adult supervision at all times.

**Older kids around 12 and up** can, in addition to the above, play with the bird in more complex ways, including taking it outside in its cage with adult supervision.

## CASE STUDY: CRAZY FOR COCKATOOS

Parents: Greg and Alison Harris
Children: Emily and Charles
San Diego, California

The first time the Harris family saw Harold was at a pet store. They were waiting on a prescription at the pharmacy, and Allison thought she would take Emily and Charles into the pet shop next door to look at the animals for a few minutes.

She thought they would go gaga for the little dogs at the front of the store, but they were fascinated by this white bird with a tall, feathery Mohawk. The sign on the bird's cage identified him as an umbrella cockatoo. The store attendant saw how interested the kids were and came over and showed them how the bird could say things, like "What is your name?" and "SpongeBob SquarePants" (obviously, someone with a good sense of humor had trained the bird).

Emily and Charles were talking about the bird all night and for the next couple of days. Greg and Allison kept expecting them to just forget about the bird, but they were completely fascinated. Emily asked if they could go back the next weekend to see the bird again so she could show her dad how cool the bird was.

Greg and Allison had talked casually about getting a pet, but they had kind of thought they would want a dog or a cat. The idea of a pet bird floored them a little — they had no experience with birds at all. Allison ended up searching "umbrella cockatoos" online and found a bird group on Meetup.com (**www.meetup.com**) in their area. They were having a meeting in about a week, so she decided to drop by, and she is glad she did, because the people there were able to give her a really good idea of what it is like to own a bird. A couple of people even offered to bring their birds over for Emily and Charles to spend time with so that they could see if a bird was a good fit.

Three months after they first spotted him, Emily and Charles got to bring Harold home from the pet store, along with a cage, plenty of birdseed, a bird bath, and so much other equipment — Allison probably would have panicked over the price tag if the bird group had not prepared her for it.

Now it is hard to imagine their family without Harold. He has learned to say all of their names and greets them enthusiastically when they come into the family room where he holds court. The whole family participates in feeding him, changing his water bottle, and making sure he gets his bath a couple of times a week. And they love their nightly "fly time" when Harold zooms around the family room from person to person.

# Chapter 6

Fish

# At a Glance

**THE BEST PART**.................
Fish come in a variety of interesting sizes, shapes, and colors, and they fit nicely into even the smallest homes.

**THE BIGGEST CHALLENGE**.....
If you are looking for a pet to play and cuddle with, you may be disappointed by the lack of interactivity in your pet fish.

**COST**..............................
Usually around $100 (but could go more or less depending on how elaborate the tank is) in start-up costs, including adoption or purchase and starter gear and about $3 a month for food and maintenance.

**NEEDS**.............................
After you have set up the tank and conditioned the water (plan on this taking a couple of hours), your fish will need to be fed and have their water changed regularly, depending on what type of fish tank and fish you own.

**AVERAGE LIFESPAN**.............
About 2 years.

At dentists' offices and restaurants, children stand spellbound in front of aquariums. There is something magical about watching colorful fish swim in crystal-clear water, which may explain why there are about 9 million pet fish in the United States, according to the American Pet Products Manufacturing Association. Fish are pleasant, low-maintenance pets that are attractive to have around and offer little to no allergy risk. Aesthetically, they offer a range of gorgeous colors that you could coordinate with your room's decor, if you so desired. As with any pet, fish come with ownership pros and cons. This chapter will look at fish and the responsibilities they entail, highlighting some of the advantages and challenges of fish ownership, as well as considering what kind of fish are best for families and how children can get involved in their pet's care.

## What Your Pet Fish Needs

Fish are among the most low maintenance pets a family can own. After the initial purchase price, monthly upkeep is minimal — both in terms of cost and effort.

### Cost

You can expect to pay around $100 in start-up costs for your fish. The fish themselves generally range in price from a few cents to a few dollars each (though of course you can spend much more on rare breeds of fish), but a standard six-fish community of tetras or mollies should cost around $16. The rest of the money goes toward the aquarium and supplies your pet fish needs to be comfortable. This includes:

- An aquarium or fish tank — 10 gallons is the recommended minimum size for controlling temperature and chemical balance for multiple fish; experts recommend one gallon of water for every inch of fish in your tank

- A water heater, if your fish requires a water temperature higher than your home's natural room temperature

- Air pump (to move air through the tank; this is necessary if you have an air pump filter or tank accessories that require circulating water to work properly)

- Foliage (for your fish to hide in)

- Water filter

- Rocks or pebbles for the bottom of the tank

- Fish food

- Snails or algae eaters for tank hygiene

- Net and small bowl(s) for removing fish to clean tank

- Tank light (depending on what type of tank you have)

After this initial outlay that may seem like a lot, fish are very affordable. You can expect to spend around $3 each month for food and other supplies, in addition to the one-time start-up costs.

## Space

Fish need minimal space — as long as you have enough surface area to safely house their tank, fish are just as comfortable in just about any-sized dwelling. One thing to keep in mind as you are making room for your fish is that fish generally prefer dimmer lights and do not require a lot of indoor light to stimulate activity.

Too much light can also overheat the water, which can be fatal to your fish. Another thing to remember is that if you live in a cold climate and adopt a tropical fish, you will probably need a water heater to keep your fish comfortable.

Though every pet requires a period of adjustment to get used to its new home, fish have very specific housing needs when it comes to their tank and there are some things you should take care to do to prepare it.

**Before you bring home your fish,** you should have your fish tank up and running for a few days because you will need to give the water in your aquarium plenty of time to fully reach room temperature. Letting the water come to room temperature does away with any chlorine in the water, which can be harmful to fish.

**When you bring home your fish,** you will want to make the transition from bag to tank as gradual as possible. Start by floating your fish's plastic bag in the fish tank until the water temperature is the same in the bag and the tank. Once they are the same temperature, add a little tank water to your fish's bag; then add a little more in about an hour. After that, it should be safe to transfer your fish from its bag to its new tank.

## Time

Just as with any pet, you should expect to spend a little time every day caring for your pet fish. But in general, fish do not require a significant time investment.

## Daily

- Feeding the fish, which only takes a few seconds to sprinkle on top of the water's surface

## Weekly

- Cleaning the tank (depends on type of fish and tank)
- Changing the water (depends on type of fish and tank)

# Cleaning

Caring for your fish's tank is a lot like grooming a furry or feathered pet: Doing it helps your fish stay healthy and active. You will not need to use cleaning products — in fact, most cleaning products should be avoided because they can be toxic to fish — but simply good old-fashioned elbow grease.

**Filter:** You should clean your fish tank's filter thoroughly every other week to once every month by following the instructions for cleaning that come with your tank. At the same time, you should clean any slime, algae or plant waste from the outside of your filter and change any activated carbon bags. You should also clean plant debris from the filter whenever you see it there.

**Hood:** Use a brush or scrubber to thoroughly clean the underside of your fish tank's hood (if it has one) once a week.

**Tank:** Scrape any algae, slime, or plant residue from the tank walls once a week. If you have a freshwater tank, you should relocate all your pet fish to temporary containers, clear the aquarium of rocks and accessories, and thoroughly clean the entire tank about once a month. This makes sure they fish are living in the healthiest environment possible. Saltwater tanks have different requirements; you should add iodine twice a week, scrape algae from the walls every week, check the filter pads every two weeks, test the alkalinity every month, and check your fish at least every three days to make sure they are healthy.

**Water:** Change some of the water in your tank each week, remembering to add only non-chlorinated, room temperature water to your tank. Rule of thumb: Change 30 percent of the water every 30 days — you can change the percentage and timeframe in whatever way is most convenient for your family. For saltwater tanks, remove 10 to 15 percent of the water weekly and replace with dechlorinated water. You should also replenish evaporated water with dechlorinated water that you have added calcium to. Once a month, you should change 25 percent of the tank water.

## Can Your Child Handle a Fish?

A fish is a pet that most children can enjoy regardless of age or habits, though depending on your particular child's age and responsibility level, you may decide to limit your child's access to your pet.

### Your child's age

If your child is old enough to resist the urge to reach into the fish tank and pull out his or her swimming friends, then your child is old enough to have a pet fish. (If you have space to keep a tank that is inaccessible to your child, then you do not have to worry about this.) Unlike many other pets, fish do not bond with the person who takes care of them, so if your child is too young to be an active participant in fish care, he or she will not miss out on the full pet experience the way he or she would with a dog or a cat. Also because fish do not bond, your child can take on pet care responsibilities as he or she matures without making it necessary to retrain your pet. If your child is very young, you may want to consider investing in an aquarium and fish that do not need a water heater, since the combination of electricity and water can be potentially harmful to small children who do not understand the dangers.

## Your child's health

Allergies are not really an issue for most people when it comes to pet fish. A very few people who are allergic to shellfish may have inhalant-based allergies, meaning that just breathing in the same area with shellfish can trigger an allergic reaction, but this is a rare condition and few fish that people consider as pets fall into the shellfish category. (Since shellfish allergies usually require a person to ingest the shellfish, aquarium fish are usually safe for people who have shellfish allergies.) If your child is very allergic to mold, you will want to be extra vigilant when it comes to tank cleaning since standing water in the tank can promote the growth of mold. In general, though, fish are the ultimate hypoallergenic pets.

## Your child's play habits

Fish tend to get stressed if their physical environment is disrupted — for instance, if you change their tank environment or their food significantly. So, if you suspect your child is likely to play "catch-the-fish" with a net very often, a fish probably is not a great pet for your family. On the other hand, fish are unlikely to be negatively impacted by children running around and shouting, which makes fish capable of fitting seamlessly into a noisy household.

## Your child's home habits

If your child will be an active participant in caring for your family's pet fish, it is important that your child be responsible enough to follow very specific directions and that you have time to carefully supervise his or her interaction with your pet. Unlike other pets where precisely measured food is not a requirement, the wrong amount of food can be toxic for fish, something any child who participates in caring for a fish needs to be responsible enough to understand. If your daughter is likely to leave lights on and doors opened, her room may not be the best place for your aquarium to be housed. If your son tends to be sloppy and careless, he may not be ready to care for a pet fish yet, though he may enjoy looking at them.

## Your child's schedule

Busy children and children who have plenty of time at home can do equally well with pet fish, since fish need little one-on-one interaction. The only daily task a pet fish requires is to be fed.

## Your child's experience with fish

Some children are disappointed with pet fish because they are not playful or cuddly pets. Fish are independent and self-contained, so be sure your child understands what pet fish are like before you bring them home.

# You are All Wet

If you are about to become the proud caretakers of an aquarium full of fish, you'll enjoy these fish facts.

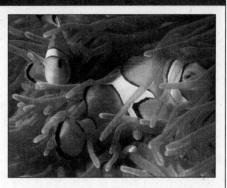

1. Fish have ears, but they do not use them to hear. Instead, they rely on vibrations and movement in the water to "hear" what is happening around them.

2. Fish do not have eyelids so they sleep with their eyes wide open. If you think you spot a fish blinking, you are probably seeing the fish spin its eyeballs.

3. A group of goldfish is called a troubling.

4. Some fish, including angelfish, mate for life.

5. A number of fish feed on insects that they leap out of the water to catch.

## Finding the Right Fish

Though fish can seem remarkably similar, there are differences in care and behavior that you will want to consider before choosing a fish as your family pet. One of the most important things to consider if you are getting an aquarium full of fish is how the different fish will get along with each other. Here are some factors you will want to bear in mind as you consider which pet is best for your family.

### Size

Like most animals, fish start out smaller and increase in size as they get older. The bigger a fish is (or will become), the more tank space it needs to live a healthy, happy life. If you are choosing one larger fish and several comparatively smaller fish, do your research to find out if the big fish is aggressive or if it eats smaller fish — watching one of your pet fish be devoured by another fish or coming home to find a dead fish can be a traumatic experience for a child.

## Sociability

A variety of fish in a tank make for the most interesting aquariums, but it is important to choose fish that live together well. Some fish are very territorial and need a large space to roam — do not choose these types of fish unless you have the tank space to give them what they want. Other fish may eat other fish or prey on smaller fish, so be careful choosing those fish to populate your tank. Consider the water level at which fish are

**Something's Fishy**

If one of your pet fish is acting sick — swimming slowly, exhibiting suspicious marks or displaying other "weird" behavior or characteristics — it is important to isolate the unhealthy fish from the rest of the aquarium in his or her own container until you can figure out what is going on.

comfortable swimming, too: Fish who feel comfortable having space on their particular level create a more sociable environment than fish fighting for space on the same level.

## Tank

If you are choosing a variety of fish for your tank, be sure to choose fish with the same tank needs. Choosing fish that need different water temperatures or pH balances makes it difficult to accommodate all your pets in one tank. You should also choose all saltwater or all freshwater fish. (Freshwater fish are generally easier for first-time fish owners to care for than saltwater fish.)

## Saltwater tank tutorial

Saltwater aquariums can be beautiful examples of ecosystems that will fascinate your family, but it is important to note that these types of aquariums require considerably more care and maintenance than regular aquariums. If your family is excited about the idea of a saltwater aquarium, here are some things to keep in mind:

- Saltwater fish need more space than freshwater fish. A 50-gallon tank is usually the smallest size for saltwater aquariums since saltwater fish need about 3 gallons of water for every inch of size (compared to freshwater fish, who need about 1 gallon of water per inch of size).

- You will need to plan on a four- to six-week initial period to establish your tank's nitrate cycle, the cycle that cleans away ammonia and waste and restores clean water to your tank. During this time, you can have only a small number of one species of fish in your tank — damselfish are often recommended.

- You will need special equipment for a saltwater tank, including spectrum lighting, a substrate of aragonite sand and live rock, a protein skimmer, a salt mix and a hydrometer.

- A saltwater tank requires more maintenance than a fresh-water tank. You will need to test the water in your saltwater aquarium regularly for salinity, calcium, nitrate, alkalinity, and pH to maintain the health of the plants and fish.

# Family-friendly Fish

There are more than 2,000 species of fish you can consider for your aquarium. Most are family-friendly, and most fish have similar needs. The fish highlighted below are some of the most popular with fish owners.

## Siamese fighting fish (Betta fish)

**What makes them family-friendly:** Most commonly known as Betta fish, these fish tend to fight amongst themselves but get along with most other species of fish, even though they have the reputation they need to be kept isolated. The males are particularly attractive fish, with long, elegant fins and dazzling scales; the females are plain brown.

**What they need from you:** Because they come from the tropics, Betta fish need a tank environment that is well heated. However, even though Betta fish get along with other species, you should limit yourself to one male Betta fish per tank, since male Betta fish are notorious for fighting with each other — they will even try to attack each other through the glass if they spot one another in separate aquariums.

## Rainbow fish

**What makes them family-friendly**: Colorful and sociable, rainbow fish live happily together in groups of six or more. They are very active, which can make them fun to watch.

**What they need from you**: Because they are larger than many other "starter" fish and do best in small groups, rainbow fish need a tank big enough to comfortably accommodate them. They will be more comfortable in a 40-gallon tank than smaller fish such as Betta fish that do just fine in a 20-gallon tank.

## Guppies

**What makes them family-friendly**: These hardy, friendly fish come in a rainbow of colors that will make it fun to choose your favorites. They also get along well with other fish, although males have been known to nip at other top-swimmers in the tank.

**What they need from you**: Guppies are very sociable, so bring them home in small groups. When you are choosing your fish, remember to choose a few of the plainer female fish as well as the vividly hued males because guppies are happiest in groups.

## Barbs

**What makes them family-friendly**: Because they are naturally hardier than other fish, barbs can survive many of the mistakes newbie tank owners make, such as the shock of sudden water changes and minimal overfeeding.

**What they need from you**: Small barbs have a tendency to nip so avoid making them the largest fish in your tank. If you want to breed your barbs, you will need to set up a separate breeding tank or risk your eggs being eaten by their prospective parents. If you plan on having them in a tank with other species of fish, make sure you have a group of six or more barbs in order to reduce the incidence of aggression towards more passive tank mates.

## Tetras

**What makes them family-friendly:** These pretty tropical fish are active and pleasant, making them prime fodder for fish observation.

**What they need from you:** Tetras thrive in groups, so a school of at least six ensures maximum fish happiness. Tetras also love plants and other tank elements for hiding, so be sure your tank has plenty of places for them to play hide-and-seek. They do best in a tank with moderate lighting.

## Common goldfish

**What makes them family friendly:** Goldfish are one of the few types of fish that actually bond with their owners, and after a few years of fish ownership, your pet fish might take food directly from your hand.

**What they need from you:** Though the goldfish swimming in its glass bowl is an iconic image for most of us, goldfish actually need a standard aquarium — complete with water temperature below 72 degrees — to thrive. Aeration is important, because they produce a lot of waste and tanks can quickly become toxic if it builds up. Goldfish are happiest living in groups with other goldfish.

# Getting Your Kids Involved

Ultimately, the responsibility for caring for any family pet belongs to the parents, but there are lots of ways children can help care for your pet fish.

## Feeding

Feeding is an everyday task for fish owners, so it is a good way to teach your children responsibility and caring skills.

**Toddlers and preschoolers** can fetch the fish food and supplies when it is feeding time and give the occasional fish treat.

**Elementary-school kids** can measure out the correct amount of food and add it to the tank, as well as the tasks younger children can handle.

**Older kids around 12 and up** can help plan special treats for your fish to help balance their overall diet, such as freeze-dried bloodworms (midge larvae) or brine shrimp, as well as helping with daily feeding.

## Cleaning

Cleaning the tank is an important part of fish ownership, and it is never too early to get your child involved.

**Toddlers and preschoolers** can help you check the tank and filter each day for visible debris. (Young children love this kind of hide-and-seek.)

**Elementary-school kids** can help with scraping and cleaning the top and sides of the tank, in addition to the daily tasks younger children handle.

**Older kids around 12 and up** can help with cleaning and changing the filter as well as the previously mentioned tasks.

## CASE STUDY: A FAMILY OF FISH

Parents: Julie and Ron Garfield
Child: Lena
Hoboken, New Jersey

When Lena was a baby, she would sit for hours transfixed in front of the aquarium, watching the six small tetras inside swim around. She especially loved feeding time, and she would giggle and clap when the fish sped through the water to grab a food flake. Julie and Ron were careful to position her where she could not reach the tank, and they made sure the aquarium was in a safe, supported location where it could not be knocked over.

Ron and Julie really wanted a pet, but between their small apartment and a new baby, they knew a high-maintenance pet was out of the question. Fish — Ron's idea, Julie thinks, originally — seemed like a perfect solution. About three months after Lena was born, Ron brought home a 20-gallon aquarium. They got it all set up and let it run for about a week before the family picked up a few snails to keep the tank clean. A few weeks later, they brought home three tetras. A few months later, they added three more tetras. Originally, they planned to include a variety of fish, but in the end they decided to save variety for later on and to keep things simple while Lena was little.

Lena is 2 years old now, so she obviously cannot do much to help with the fish, but she loves spending time watching them. She especially loves once a month when they take all the fish out and line them up in separate bowls to clean the aquarium.

Taking care of the fish is easy. The Garfields feed them twice a day and clean the tank once a week, with a complete cleaning session once a month or so. They have lost two fish and replaced them. They change the tank up seasonally: They put a little Christmas tree in the tank for the holidays, and they have a beach umbrella in the summer. It is silly but fun — probably like other people buying their dog a sweater. When they go out of town, they pay their 13-year-old neighbor $5 a day to come feed the fish. The Garfields travel a lot so having pets that do not need special care while they are gone is a real plus.

# Chapter 7

Other Small Pets

Though dogs, cats, birds, and fish are the pets people think of most often, they are far from being the only pets for families to choose from. There are dozens of other small pets (sometimes referred to as "exotics") that families can bring home. In this section, we will focus on several of the most popular small pets, including small rodents (guinea pigs, hamsters, gerbils and mice), lizards and other reptiles, and rabbits.

## Guinea Pigs

### At a Glance

| | |
|---|---|
| **THE BEST PART**................... | Guinea pigs are cute and fun. |
| **THE BIGGEST CHALLENGE**..... | These little rodents have a lot of specific needs and are easily stressed. |
| **COST**........................... | Usually around $100 or more in start-up costs, including adoption or purchase price and starter gear and about $25 a month for food and maintenance. |

**NEEDS**........................... In addition to daily feeding, your guinea pig will need his or her cage lining changed at least two times a week. Long-haired guinea pigs also need regular grooming. In addition, guinea pigs are very social animals that do best in same-sex pairs, so you should consider getting two.

**AVERAGE LIFESPAN**............. About 5 years.

Guinea pigs may be small — most do not get bigger than about 2 pounds — but these cute little balls of fur are fairly high-maintenance pets for a small animal. Though they require a lot of attention, they are sweet and playful.

## Cost

Expect to pay around $100 in start-up costs for your pet guinea pig. In addition to the adoption fee or purchase price (which can range from $10 to $35, depending on the type of guinea pig you adopt), you will need to invest in all the gear your guinea pig needs to be comfortable. This includes:

- A cage
- Cage bedding
- Food pellets
- Food container
- Water container
- Hay
- Harness to take guinea pig for walks
- Exercise ball and other toys

Guinea pigs also add to your monthly expenses. You can expect to spend around $25 each month for food (pellets and fresh fruit and vegetables), hay, and bedding, in addition to the one-time, start-up costs.

## Space

Guinea pigs may not be large animals, but they are very active and need a substantial amount of space to stay healthy and happy. Though cages come in smaller sizes, Cavy Spirit (**www.cavyspirit.com**), an organization that promotes guinea pig welfare, recommends 10 ½ square feet as the minimum cage size for guinea pigs. You will need to be sure you have a comfortable, central space in your home to keep your guinea pig — because they are social animals, guinea pigs do not like to be relegated to lonely corners of your home. Guinea pigs also need floor space to roll around and play, so you will need to take that into account when you are considering a guinea pig as a pet. Most guinea pigs also enjoy outside time on a harness, so a pedestrian-friendly neighborhood or backyard is a plus. Since guinea pigs are so small, walking them in heavily congested urban areas can be dangerous.

## Time

Guinea pigs need a lot of time and attention. People often think of guinea pigs as "starter pets" that do not require a lot of care, but adopting a guinea pig is almost as much work as adopting a cat or dog, which is something to keep in mind as you are making your decision.

### Daily
- Feed guinea pig twice
- Prepare for playtime on the floor
- Spend at least one hour playing with guinea pig
- Clean up after playing

## Weekly

- Refresh cage hay three times
- Partially clean cage once
- Thoroughly clean cage once

## Grooming

Like cats, guinea pigs take care of most of their grooming themselves. Still, there are times when owners should step in to help.

**Washing:** If your guinea pig has gotten into something sticky or his or her fur is matted, your guinea pig may need a bath. Otherwise, guinea pigs keep themselves clean much the same way that cats do — though, unlike cats, guinea pigs usually enjoy the occasional bath.

**Brushing:** Medium- and long-haired guinea pigs do well with occasional brushing. Short-haired guinea pigs generally do not need brushing but may enjoy being brushed.

## Characteristics

Guinea pigs tend to have the same general size and shape, so many people are surprised to learn that there are actually 13 distinct types of guinea pig, each with different characteristics and personality traits. Some of the most family friendly are:

**American**: With short, easy-to-maintain hair and tons of personality, American guinea pigs love children — as long as the children understand how to be careful with them. American guinea pigs are the most common — in some pet stores, they might be called English guinea pigs.

**Teddy**: Among the more recent breeds of guinea pigs, Teddy guinea pigs get their name from their resemblance to teddy bears. Their round, furry bodies and sweet, docile personalities make these adorable guinea pigs great for families with children.

# 5 Things You Should Know about Guinea Pigs

1. Guinea pigs are officially known as cavies and were originally domesticated in ancient South American by the Inca tribe.

2. Guinea pigs may be called "guinea pigs" because they cost a guinea in British shops or because they originally came to Europe from Dutch Guinea in South American during the colonial period.

3. Guinea pigs love crunchy vegetables, such as carrots and broccoli.

4. A guinea pig can run when it is as young as three hours old.

5. Because they do not have musk glands like other rodents, guinea pigs are one of the least smelly caged pet options.

## Is your child ready for a guinea pig?

According the Cavy Spirit Web site, kids between ages 9 and 11 are the perfect age to embrace a guinea pig as their family pet. The reason: By 9, most children are responsible enough to understand that pets are not toys and to treat fragile guinea pigs gently and respectful. Children that age are also likely to be living at home for the lifespan of their pet, preventing the likelihood of the pet being abandoned when they go off to college. That does not mean a guinea pig is automatically out of bounds as a pet for people with younger or older children, but between 9 and 11 is the optimum age for kids in families with pet guinea pigs.

Guinea pig allergies are caused by proteins in the guinea pig's saliva and urine rather than in its fur or dander, and a simple test at the doctor's office or an allergist's office can determine whether your child is allergic. The hay and bedding in your guinea pig's cage may also trigger allergies: You can help minimize this by cleaning the cage outside and changing the bedding regularly so that your guinea pigs have only as much bedding as they need to completely cover their cage floor at a given time.

Children who play rough and have not developed a sense of caution with fragile things probably are not ready to have a guinea pig as a pet. On the other hand, children who are careful and responsible and love to play with small toys such may truly appreciate and enjoy a delicate guinea pig. At home, if your child has trouble remembering to clean up after him or herself and shows a lack of respect for the items in your home, she will have trouble caring for a small, sensitive pet like a guinea pig. If, however, he or she is responsible and careful, a guinea pig might be the right pet for your family.

Guinea pigs are very social creatures that need plenty of time to play and bond with their owners. If your child's schedule is too hectic to permit much leisure home time, it may not be a good idea for your family to adopt a guinea pig. In contrast, guinea pigs are a wonderful addition to a family who spends a lot of time at home together. If your family frequently takes long trips, be sure you have a plan in place for your guinea pig. Guinea pigs need more care than fish, but there are few kennels and pet sitters that specialize in caring for them. It can also be a challenge to find hotels and accommodations that allow guinea pigs.

As with any pet, guinea pigs will rely on the adults for most of their care. But there are plenty of ways children can get involved in caring for the family guinea pig.

## Feeding

Feeding can be a great way to help your child bond with your guinea pig.

**Toddlers and preschoolers** can help put out food for guinea pigs.

**Elementary-school kids** can measure the correct amount of food and help with shopping for fruits and vegetables to supplement the guinea pig's diet.

**Older kids around 12 and up** can help wash and dry food containers, as well as the above activities.

## Grooming

Guinea pigs do not need a lot of grooming, but it is a good bonding opportunity and a way for your child to learn how to be gentle with your pet guinea pig. Until your children are teenagers or you feel 100 percent confident in their responsibility, all grooming should be actively supervised by adults.

**Toddlers and preschoolers** should not be allowed to groom guinea pigs.

**Elementary-school kids** can gently brush the guinea pig while an adult holds it.

**Older kids around 12 and up** can hold and brush a guinea pig with adult supervision.

## Cleaning

Cage maintenance is an important part of owning a guinea pig, so get your kids involved early.

**Toddlers and preschoolers** can help with weekly cage cleaning.

**Elementary-school kids** can help change the cage lining and bedding with adult supervision, as well as helping with weekly cage cleaning.

**Older kids around 12 and up** can help with daily cage cleaning and take responsibility for the weekly cage cleaning sessions.

## Playing

Guinea pigs need plenty of playtime, but an adult should always be around to make sure things do not get out of hand.

**Toddlers and preschoolers** can help set out and clean up toys before and after the guinea pig's playtime and play with the animal with adult supervision. Young children should not pick up guinea pigs by themselves, but they can carefully hold a guinea pig if an adult hands it to them and stays close to be sure the guinea pig is safe.

**Elementary-school kids** can help set up toy obstacle courses for the guinea pigs during playtime and play with the guinea pig with adult supervision, in addition to the responsibilities above.

**Older kids around 12 and up** can do all of the above, plus learn how to take the guinea pig outside on its harness.

# Rats

## At a Glance

| | |
|---|---|
| THE BEST PART.................. | Rats are clever and playful. They are very responsive to training and love to cuddle. |
| THE BIGGEST CHALLENGE..... | Because they are nocturnal, rats are less active during the day and can be noisy at night. |
| COST........................... | Usually around $100 or more in startup costs, including adoption or purchase and starter gear and about $25 a month for food and maintenance. |
| NEEDS........................... | Rats need plenty of playtime — plan on at least an hour a day — plus daily feeding and cage cleanup. Their cages need to be completely cleaned once a week. |
| AVERAGE LIFESPAN............. | 2–3 years. |

Thanks in part to the animated movie Ratatouille, pet rats have seen a recent surge in popularity, while in the past have experienced plenty of unfair prejudice because of their undomesticated relatives. Just as domesticated dogs are completely different from wild dogs, domesticated rats have little in common with wild rats and can make great pets for the right family.

## Cost

Expect to pay around $100 in start-up costs for your pet rat. This includes the purchase price or adoption fee for your rat, as well as the gear your rat will need, including:

- Cage (12x24 inches is the recommended cage size) with a covered area
- Water bottle
- Food container
- Rat food
- Cage liner
- Chew toys and other toys, such as tunnels and play tubes

You should also expect to pay around $25 in monthly expenses for your rat, including food and fresh cage lining.

## Space

Rats are playful, but they do not need a ton of room, making them an ideal pet for tight spaces. They will need a safe spot for their cage and a secured area for their daily playtime, but it is not difficult to make room for them. Pet rats should stay indoors, so outdoor space is not necessary for these pets.

## Time

Rats are fairly low-maintenance pets. Because they sleep most of the day, a busy schedule can be a plus for pet rats.

### Daily

- Feed rat
- Play with rat for at least one hour out of cage

### Weekly

- Clean cage thoroughly (or more frequently, as needed)
- Change cage liner (or more frequently, as needed)
- Grooming, if needed and only as needed

## Grooming

For the most part, rats groom themselves, but occasionally, they may need a little help from their owners.

**Washing:** If your rat's fur becomes matted or sticky, it may be time for a bath. Use a very small amount of gentle shampoo formulated for small animals — you can ask your vet for a recommendation — and rinse thoroughly.

## Characteristics

There are a few exotic breeds of rats (such as Russian blues or English minks), but for the most part, common rats are very similar. Considering these factors will help you choose the one that is right for your particular family.

**Male Rats** (also called bucks) are larger than females and more affectionate. They tend to love petting and cuddling time. On the downside, they are very territorial and tend to mark their territory in the time-honored tradition of urinating all over their cages, meaning their cage might need more frequent cleaning than a female.

**Female Rats** (called does) are more active and playful but less cuddly than their male counterparts. They are also more likely to try to wriggle away and hide when you remove them from their cages.

Because rats have a fairly short lifespan, most people tend to choose younger rats to maximize their family's time with their pets. Also, it is not easy to quantify personality traits, but in general, look for a rat that is active and alert, even curious, and one who does not panic when gently approached or held.

## 5 Things You Should Know about Rats

1. Rats use all the tiny hairs on their long tails as a personal climate control system: The hairs help them warm up and cool down.

2. Rats do not see very well, so they will learn to recognize their owners by voice and smell. Encourage your children to talk to their pet rat when they are near its cage so that the rat becomes familiar with their voice.

3. Curious about the age of your

rat? Check its head: Rats younger than 6 months tend to have small, pointy heads; as rats get older, their hats get wider and flatter.

4. Female rats can reproduce as many as six times a year, so keep same-sex pairs unless you want rat babies.

5. Rats have delicately balanced systems and can become seriously ill or die if you use the wrong kind of shavings in their cage. Avoid pine shavings, cedar shavings, and other softwood shavings, which cause respiratory tract damage. Ask your vet to recommend the best shavings for your pet.

## Is your child ready for a rat?

Because rats are small, very young children can injure them easily —and unintentionally. Most children can pet and play with a rat by the time they are about 5 years old, but if your 4-year-old is very mature or your 7-year-old is particularly prone to roughhousing, you should take that into consideration when deciding whether a pet rat is right for your family.

Allergies to rats are common — like other furry animals, rats can cause allergies with pet hair and dander. If your child is prone to animal allergies and you have your heart set on a pet rat, be sure you give your child an opportunity to spend time around other pet rats before you bring home one of your own so that you can check reactions. If you do not know anyone who has a pet rat, contact your local rat rescue group or pet club to see if you can make arrangements for your child to spend time around a pet rat. If your child does have an allergic reaction after spending time with a rat, it is possible that he or she is allergic to the rat's bedding rather than to the rat itself. Your child's pediatrician or an allergy specialist can also give your child a fairly simple test to gauge your child's allergies to rats.

Because rats are small, they do not do well with children who have a tendency to play rough — a rambunctious child could easily injure a small rat without meaning to hurt it or provoke a frightened rat into biting. If your child is careful with his or her toys and plays with small toys without breaking them, a pet rat could thrive in your family.

Rats are clever animals that can be easily trained, so it is important for them to have consistent care and instructions — otherwise, you lose the benefits of being able to train them. If your child forgets to do his or her chores and needs lots of reminders to do his or her homework or clean up his or her room, you should expect to take on the brunt of the duties. If your child is very messy, a rat may not be a good pet for your family since rats love to hide in piles and to chew anything in sight — including electrical wires and toys.

Rats need an hour of playtime each day, but because they are nocturnal animals, they are great pets for kids with busy schedules. Rats keep to themselves most of the day and perk up when evening falls — about the same time most busy kids are coming home. (Because they are awake at night, you may want to make sure your pet rat's cage is not in a place where your pet's nocturnal antics will interfere with your family's sleep.) If your days are very busy, adopting two rats might be a good idea since rats are social animals and can keep each other company.

As it has been stressed before, the primary responsibility for caring for a pet falls on the parents, but there are many ways a child can help care for a pet rat.

## Feeding

**Toddlers and preschoolers** can help dry the feeding and water bowls and help put out food for their pet with adult supervision.

**Elementary-school kids** can do those things; they can also learn how to give your rat hand-held snacks with help from adults.

**Older kids around 12 and up** can feed and water your pet rat and clean his or her feeding and water bowls, in addition to the above responsibilities.

## Cleaning

**Toddlers and preschoolers** can help prepare and place new liners in the cage.

**Elementary-school kids** can help with cage cleaning, as well as with new liners.

**Older kids around 12 and up** can learn how to clean the cage and remove and change the cage liners, in addition to the duties above.

## Playing

**Toddlers and preschoolers** can help set out and clean up toys before and after the rat's playtime and play with the animal with adult supervision.

**Elementary-school kids** can learn how to train their pet rat with treats and play with it with adult supervision, in addition to helping with playtime toys.

**Older kids around 12 and up** can do all of the above and also teach their pet tricks, such as navigating mazes.

# Hamsters

## At a Glance

| | |
|---|---|
| **THE BEST PART**................. | Playful and affordable, hamsters can make themselves comfortable in a fairly small space and do not need much one-on-one time to be happy. |
| **THE BIGGEST CHALLENGE**..... | Because they are nocturnal, hamsters sleep most of the day and can make a lot of noise at night. They are also unhappy about being awakened during the day and may nip the person who wakes them. |
| **COST**............................ | Usually around $60 or more in start-up costs, including adoption or purchase and starter gear and about $20 a month for food and maintenance. |
| **NEEDS**........................... | Hamsters need daily feeding and cage clean up and thrive on daily playtime with their owners. |
| **AVERAGE LIFESPAN**............ | 2–3 years. |

Hamsters are cute, cuddly pets whose playful antics delight most kids. They are also fairly low-maintenance pets, which makes them a popular choice for many school classrooms.

## Cost

Expect to pay around $60 in start-up costs for your pet hamster. In addition to the purchase or adoption cost of your pet hamster, you will need to stock up with the supplies he or she needs to live a healthy, happy hamster life:

- A cage (At least 10 gallons is the recommended size)
- Bedding, such as Timothy hay or aspen shavings
- Exercise wheel
- Play tubes
- Food tray
- Attachable water bottle
- Chew toys
- Hand glove for picking up a new hamster

The biggest cost for a hamster's monthly upkeep is replacing the cage bedding, so keep an eye out for bulk discounts. In general, expect to pay about $20 a month for your pet hamster — about $2 for food and $18 for bedding.

## Time

Hamsters love attention, but they are also pretty good at entertaining themselves. The biggest time commitment to a pet hamster is the daily cleaning their living area requires.

### Daily

- Feed hamster several small meals
- Clean cage bedding
- Play with hamster

### Weekly

- Thoroughly clean cage, at least once a week or as needed
- Replace cage lining, at least once a week or as needed

## Space and grooming

If you have room for at least a 10-gallon container, you have plenty of room for a hamster. Keep in mind that hamsters are awake and active for most of the night, so unless you are a very sound sleeper, it is a good idea to keep your pet hamster out of the bedrooms. Hamsters also need very little grooming as long as you keep their cage area clean. If your hamster's fur does become matted or dirty, check with your vet about the best way to clean your hamster.

## Breeds

**Syrian hamsters:** Also called black bear hamsters, golden hamsters, teddy bear hamsters, and fancy hamsters, Syrian hamsters are the largest hamsters (growing to between 6 and 8 inches) and have pretty, golden coats with dark brown markings. Because they are territorial, they are happiest  being alone in their cages with no other hamsters. They are generally tame and playful and get very active in the late afternoon and early evening.

**Dwarf hamsters:** Dwarf hamsters come in several varieties including Campbell's Russian hamsters, Winter White Russian hamsters, and Roborovski hamsters, and grow to only about 4 or 5 inches in length. These hamsters are happiest in pairs, but choose same-sex pairs if you do not want hamster babies. They are docile and playful.

# 5 Things You Should Know about Hamsters

1. The word "hamster" comes from the German word "to hoard" — and that is exactly what your pet hamster will do with any food it happens to come across, so it is important to check its cage for food stashes and get rid of them.

2. Hamsters love to shred things, so a small paper towel will keep them happy for hours.

3. Hamsters' teeth grow constantly, which is why it is so important for them to have non-toxic chew toys in their cages at all times.

4. Hamsters have been popular pets since the 1930s.

5. Hamsters cannot be spayed or neutered so if you adopt an opposite sex pair, be prepared for baby hamsters.

## Is your child ready for a hamster?

Like most small pets, hamsters do best with children who are old enough and who have enough manual dexterity to handle them without hurting them. Very young children may enjoy watching hamsters play in their cage, but they should never be allowed to handle hamsters by themselves. Many younger children's classrooms have pet hamsters; if your child is one of them, your child has probably already learned about how to care responsibly for a hamster and may be ready for one of his or her own.

Allergies to rodents are fairly common but not all rodents generate the same reactions, so if your child is allergic to a rat or guinea pig, it does not necessarily follow that he or she will be allergic to a hamster. The best way to check for potential hamster allergies in your child is to let her spend some time with another pet hamster and watch her closely; a doctor or allergist can also do an allergy screening to check for allergies. Some people are allergic to the hay or shavings in hamster's bedding; trying different brands might alleviate reactions in your particular child.

Follow the usual small pet guidelines when evaluating your child's readiness for a hamster: Does he or she play rough? Does he or she frequently break his or her toys? Do you have to remind him or her to calm down and be gentle? Frightened hamsters are likely to bite, and hamsters are small and easily injured by children who are just playing hard. If your child is dangerous around breakables, a hamster might not be the best pet for this time in your family's life.

Hamsters are generally easy-going animals, but they react badly when they are frightened or if someone wakes them up in the middle of their daytime sleep. If your child has trouble remembering house rules, he or she might also have trouble remembering how to keep the family pet from freaking out. Hamsters also do not do well in homes with very messy children, since they love to sneak away and hide, and a messy room can make them hard to find. Use the prospect of a pet hamster to help your child keep a neater room or wait until your child develops better cleaning habits to bring home a hamster.

Because hamsters are nocturnal, they will not mind if the family is busy and unavailable for most of the day as long as they get some playtime in the evenings, making them a great pet for kids whose schedules are too hectic for time-intensive pets like dogs and cats.

Your child can help care for pet hamsters in many of the same ways he or she would care for a pet rat, though the ultimate responsibility for caring for any pet is, of course, the parents'.

## Feeding

**Toddlers and preschoolers** can help fill feeding and water bowls and help put out food for their pet with adult supervision.

**Elementary-school kids** can do those things, and can also learn how to give a hamster hand-held snacks with help from adults.

**Older kids around 12 and up** can feed and water a pet hamster and clean its feeding and water bowls, in addition to the above responsibilities.

## Cleaning

**Toddlers and preschoolers** can help prepare and place new liners in the cage.

**Elementary-school kids** can help with cage cleaning, as well as with new liners.

**Older kids around 12 and up** can learn how to clean the cage and remove and change the cage liners, in addition to the duties above.

## Playing

**Toddlers and preschoolers** can help set out and clean up toys before and after the hamster's playtime and play with the animal with adult supervision. It is not a good idea to let kids this age pick up a hamster by themselves, but they can gently hold them one handed with an adult.

**Elementary-school kids** can learn how to train their pet hamster with treats and play with it with adult supervision, in addition to helping with playtime toys.

**Older kids around 12 and up** can do all of the above, and also teach their pet tricks.

CASE STUDY: A CARETAKER UNTIL THE END

Parent: Karen Whiting
Child: Daniel
Baltimore, Maryland

Daniel wanted a small pet, so he went to the library and checked out all the books he could find on different kinds of small pets: hamsters, gerbils, cats, and mice. The idea of mice did not set too well with mom Karen, and he did not like cats, so he ended up deciding on a long-haired hamster as the perfect pet.

The Whitings thought they were prepared for a hamster — they bought the cage and supplies before Daniel brought his new pet home — but they were shocked and surprised when the hamster they bought died two days after they got him from wet tail, an intestinal condition that is usually fatal. The store gave them a replacement hamster at no charge, but they just were not expecting anything like that to happen.

Daniel's new hamster made a great pet. They were not surprised when he figured out a way to escape from his cage and managed to stay hidden for two days (they caught him because he made a lot of noise moving around during the night). Daniel trained his pet to come when he called, so after that, it was not hard to get the hamster back when he got away from his cage.

Daniel and his hamster really bonded, and for Karen, that was great to see. They spent hours together every day. The hamster would ride around on Daniel's shoulder or in his pocket.

Karen knew Daniel's hamster was getting old after a couple of years when he started to get big, greenish bumps on his skin, and the vet told them he was dying of old age. Daniel was amazing caring for the hamster. Daniel had to modify the hamster's cage because his feet were getting caught between the bars. The hamster had to have a special shampoo because his skin stopped producing oils. Daniel washed him in a plastic colander. When the hamster started losing hair, Daniel wrapped him in an old washcloth and gently rocked him for hours every day — he did this for the last two weeks of the hamster's life. It was sad but beautiful to see how much he cared for his pet.

# Gerbils

## At a Glance

**THE BEST PART..................** Gerbils are sweet and playful — and unlike many small animals, they are active and awake during the day. They are also curious and seldom bite. And since they are desert animals, they require significantly less cage cleaning than other rodents do.

**THE BIGGEST CHALLENGE.....** Frisky little gerbils are surprisingly good at sneaking out of their cages, so it is important to make sure they are securely enclosed.

| | |
|---|---|
| **COST**........................... | Usually around $100 or more in start-up costs, including adoption or purchase and starter gear and about $25 a month for food and maintenance. |
| **NEEDS**........................... | Gerbils need daily feeding and play-time as well as regular cage cleaning. |
| **AVERAGE LIFESPAN**............ | 3–4 years. |

Gerbils are fun, friendly pets who love to play and who can hardly contain their curiosity. These fairly low-maintenace rodents can make great family pets.

## Cost

Expect to pay around $60 in start-up costs for your gerbil. In addition to the purchase or adoption cost of your pet gerbil, you will need to stock up with the supplies he or she needs to live a healthy, happy hamster life:

- A cage or container (10 gallons is the recommended minimum size)
- Gerbil food
- Wood shavings, for bedding and digging
- Exercise wheel, play tubes, and other toys
- Attachable water bottle
- Chew toys

The biggest cost for a gerbil's monthly upkeep is replacing the cage bedding, so keep an eye out for bulk discounts. In general, expect to pay about $20 a month for your pet gerbil — about $2 for food and $18 for bedding.

## Space and grooming

If you have room for at least a 10-gallon container, you have plenty of room for a gerbil. Since gerbils are active during the day and sleep at night, it is a good idea to house them where the action is in one of the family common rooms so that they feel like part of the family. Gerbils also need almost no grooming as long as their cage does not get too dirty. If you do notice that your gerbil's coat has become matted or dirty, check with your vet about the best way to clean your gerbil.

## Time

Gerbils love attention, but they are also pretty good at entertaining themselves — especially if you adopt a pair of gerbils instead of a single one.

### Daily

- Feed the gerbil
- Replace soiled bedding with fresh bedding
- Play with the gerbil

### Weekly

- Thoroughly clean cage as needed
- Replace cage lining as needed

## Characteristics

When choosing a pet gerbil, here are some decisions you will need to make regarding what kind of gerbil is right for your family.

**Number:** Because gerbils are social animals, they do well in pairs, but only if you adopt two young gerbils at the same time (stick to same-sex pairs unless you want to have baby gerbils). If you do have a pair of gerbils, it is important to keep them together — even a few days of separation can lead to  nasty fighting in your gerbil cage when they are back together.

**Personality:** When you are choosing a gerbil, look for one that is friendly and curious — a curious gerbil will sniff your hands and crawl around them. Do not choose gerbils that cower in a corner or who nip at your hands — they are not likely to do well with kids.

# 5 Things You Should Know about Gerbils

1. Gerbils prefer to sleep in a small, enclosed space, so put a small box or flowerpot in their cage for bedtime.

2. Be sure to choose toys, tubes, and exercise wheels without slats for your pet gerbil, since its long tail can easily get caught in an opening.

3. Gerbils' teeth grow constantly, which is why it is so important for them to have non-toxic chew toys in their cages at all times.

4. In addition to gerbil food, gerbils enjoy leafy greens as an occasional treat. Just be sure to clean out any leftovers before they rot.

5. You should never hold a gerbil by its tail. Doing so could cause the skin to slip off, leaving the bone exposed and requiring the tail to be amputated.

## Is your child ready for a gerbil?

Like most small pets, gerbils do best with children who are old enough and who have enough manual dexterity to handle them without hurting them. Very young children may enjoy watching gerbils play in their cage, but they should never be allowed to handle them by themselves. Older kids who can appreciate a gerbil's playfulness and remember to be careful when handling their pet do well with pet gerbils.

Allergies to rodents are fairly common, but not all rodents generate the same reactions so if your child is allergic to a hamster or guinea pig, it does not necessarily follow that he or she will be allergic to a gerbil. The best way to check for potential gerbil allergies in your child is to let her spend some time with another pet gerbil and watch her closely; a doctor or allergist can also do an allergy screening to check for allergies. Some people are allergic to the shavings in gerbil's bedding; trying different brands might alleviate reactions in your particular child.

Follow the usual small pet guidelines when evaluating your child's readiness for a gerbil: Does he or she play rough? Does he or she frequently break his or her toys? Do you have to remind him or her to calm down and be gentle? Gerbils are small and easily injured by children who are just playing hard. If your child is dangerous around breakables, a gerbil might not be the best pet for this time in your family's life.

Quick, high-jumping gerbils are pros at making a break for it when their cages are opened, so a messy room can provide a few too many hiding places. Gerbils do best in homes where kids are reasonably neat, so use the prospect of a pet gerbil to motivate your child to clean his or her room or save getting a pet gerbil until your child is ready to tackle the responsibility of regular room clean-ups.

Unlike many small rodents, gerbils are diurnal (awake during the day), so they are great pets for a home where people are active during the day. Since they sleep during the night, they are also good pets for homes where there are light sleepers. Gerbils do not need a lot of one-on-one attention to be happy, especially if you adopt a pair of them, so they can be a good choice for children who really want a cuddly pet are too busy to take on the day-to-day responsibilities of a high-maintenance pet such as a dog or a cat.

Your child can help care for pet gerbil in many of the same ways he or she would care for a pet hamster, though the ultimate responsibility for caring for any pet belongs to the parents.

## Feeding

**Toddlers and preschoolers** can help fill feeding and water bowls and help put out food for their pet with adult supervision.

**Elementary-school kids** can do those things; they can also learn how to give your gerbil hand-held snacks with help from adults.

**Older kids around 12 and up** can feed and water your pet gerbil and clean its feeding and water bowls, in addition to the above responsibilities.

## Cleaning

**Toddlers and preschoolers** can help prepare and place new liners in the cage.

**Elementary-school kids** can help with cage cleaning, as well as with new liners.

**Older kids around 12 and up** can learn how to clean the cage and remove and change the cage liners, in addition to the duties above.

## Playing

**Toddlers and preschoolers** can help set out and clean up toys before and after the gerbil's playtime and play with the animal with adult supervision. It is not a good idea to let children this age pick up a hamster by themselves, but they can gently hold one that is handed to them by an adult.

**Elementary-school kids** can learn how to train their pet gerbil with treats and play with it with adult supervision, in addition to helping with playtime toys.

Older kids around 12 and up can do all of the above, and also teach their pet tricks.

## Lizards and Other Reptiles

# At a Glance

**THE BEST PART**.................... Reptiles are fascinating pets that can educate children about other species. Many of them need feeding only once a week and can be left on their own for several days at a time.

**THE BIGGEST CHALLENGE**..... Creating a hospitable habitat for your pet reptile requires and investment of time and effort. Some reptiles eat live animals, which can be hard for kids (and parents) handle. Reptiles can also spread salmonella.

**COST**.......................... Usually around $150 or more in start-up costs, including adoption or purchase and starter gear and about $25 a month for food and maintenance.

**NEEDS**........................... Regular feeding — how often depends on the particular reptile you choose — as well as adequate heat and exposure to full-spectrum light.

**AVERAGE LIFESPAN**............. Varies.

Make no bones about it: Reptiles can be among the most difficult pets for families to bring home. Not only is there a high cost to prepare their living space since reptiles have completely different climate needs and food requirements from mammals, reptiles also require a significant "ick" tolerance. If your family is considering a reptile as a "fallback" pet if a dog or bird is out of the question, you probably should not adopt a reptile because it is a serious commitment of time and energy to keep your pet reptile healthy and happy. If, however, you are excited about the idea of owning a pet reptile and ready and willing to take on the challenges of reptile ownership, a reptile can be a fun and rewarding family pet.

# Cost

Expect to pay around $150 in start-up costs for a pet reptile. Reptiles themselves are not that expensive — it is possible to purchase a pet snake for as little as $20 — but they require a lot of equipment, including:

- A secure, lockable enclosure of sufficient size to house your pet reptile (depending on the pet, you may need anywhere from a 10-gallon to a 60-gallon tank)
- Flooring (carpet or Astroturf) and tank bedding (shavings or newspaper shreds)
- Hide boxes or caves
- Branches, logs or other structures for climbing
- Under-tank heater
- Overhead radiant heater (ideally, one for daytime use and one for night)
- UVA- and UVB-producing fluorescent light and fixture (depending on your particular reptile's needs; check with a vet)
- Water bowl
- Feeding bowl (to remove food your reptile might not eat)
- Food: frozen or live mice for carnivorous reptiles, farm-raised insects for insectivores or dark green, leafy vegetables for herbivores (expect to pay between $.50 and $2 per mouse)
- Cleaning and disinfecting supplies

You will need to invest in both an under- and over-head tank heater in order to localize temperatures in the tank. The last thing your pet reptile needs is a "hot spot." Reptiles need food, clean bedding, and new light bulbs every month, so expect a monthly expenditure of about $25 for reptile food and maintenance.

## Space

Reptiles need a significant amount of space even though they are small creatures: The average size of reptile cage is about 20 gallons. Because they spend most of their time in their cage or enclosure, it is essential that their enclosure comfortably accommodate their size, both at the time of adoption and when they reach their full adult size. You will need to have place to house your pet reptile's enclosure. Most reptiles also need serious help with climate control, including heaters and special lights, since many are desert creatures that cannot easily adapt to more temperate climates.

## Time

Once you have adequately provided for your reptile's space and climate needs, your pet reptile is likely to need minimal upkeep.

### Daily

- Make sure your pet has fresh water

### Weekly

- Feed your pet, at least once a week or more often as needed; check with a vet about your pet's specific needs
- Thoroughly clean and disinfect your pet's enclosure; your pet's container may need intermittent cleaning as well
- Replace your pet's enclosure flooring

## Grooming

Pet reptiles usually do not need grooming, but your pet may need help during shedding time. Many reptiles, including lizards and snakes, shed their outer skin as they grow. During this time, reptiles may be particularly snappish and prone to biting, since part of the shedding process limits their vision.

To help your pet reptile during shedding periods, make sure there is plenty of fresh water in your pet's cage and create an environment that is as humid as possible because humidity promotes smooth shedding. Optimally, shedding takes place in a single piece, but if conditions are too dry, your pet may shed in smaller pieces. Either way is perfectly normal. Be sure to check your pet reptile's eyes after shedding to make sure that there are no lingering eye caps, or eye scales, remaining from the old skin. These can cause infections if left. Visit a veterinarian if the eye scales remain after shedding is completed; you should not attempt to remove the eye scales yourself.

## Common pet reptiles

There are hundreds of reptiles to choose from, but the ones listed below are some of the most common and family-friendly options.

### Leopard gecko lizards

These relatively small, nocturnal lizards manage to bypass many of the biggest challenges to reptile owners: They do not need a huge amount of space since they do not grow to enormous sizes, and they do not need special lights since they are active during

the night. And since they are docile and easy to tame, leopard gecko lizards make great family pets. They can live for 20 years or longer.

**What they need**: A 15- to 20-gallon container lined with carpet or paper (sand and shavings are not good for geckos); feeding of six to 10 calcium-coated, nutrient-loaded crickets every other day; fresh water every day; regular cage cleaning as needed.

## Bearded dragon lizards

For families who are ready and willing to embrace all the challenges of reptile ownership, bearded dragon lizards can be incredibly satisfying reptile pets. They are one of the most interesting reptiles to observe, exhibiting numerous fascinating behaviors, and are easy-to-tame, social lizards that  genuinely seem to enjoy being part of a family. Generally, bearded dragon lizards live for about 10 years.

**What they need**: At least a 40-gallon tank or container, but experts recommend choosing a container that is 55 gallons or more lined with paper or carpet rather than sand, shavings, or any liner that the bearded dragon lizard could intentionally or inadvertently swallow; UVA and UVB bulbs and fixtures; occasional exposure to sunlight; a regular daytime temperature of 80 to 85 degrees, a basking spot with a temperature of between 95 and 105 degrees, and a nighttime temperature of 65 to 70 degrees; fresh water every day; once-a-day feedings of farm-raised insects, such as crickets that have been coated with calcium and loaded with nutrients, as well as leafy green vegetables (which should make up a recommended 20 to 30 percent of the bearded dragon lizard's total diet); regular nail trimming for their claws.

## CoRn snakes

Corn snakes come in a variety of colors and patterns that make them a pleasure to look at, but it is their relatively easy care and genial personalities that make them a good choice for families planning to bring home a pet snake. Corn snakes can grow to be as long as 6 feet, but most corn snakes are

between 4 and 5 feet. They typically live for 15 to 20 years.

**What they need**: A 20-gallon, long container with secure closures — corn snakes are notorious for breaking out of their cages — bedding of newspaper, carpet, or aspen shavings and including a couple of hiding spots; a regular daytime temperature gradient in their cage between 70 and 85 degrees, with only half the tank heated so that there is temperature variety in their enclosure; fresh water every day; one pre-killed mice or rat every seven to 10 days.

## Ball pythons

Since they grow to be much shorter than other constricting snakes — most reaching their full length at between 3 and 5 feet — ball pythons are a more manageable size than longer snakes. They are docile and easy to handle. Most ball pythons live very long lives,

usually between 20 and 30 years and some for as long as 50 years, so a ball python can be a lifelong commitment.

**What they need:** At least a 30-gallon tank with a securely closing top so the ball python cannot escape; a lining of artificial grass, shredded bark, or newspaper; climbing branches; a hiding place; a regular daytime temperature between 80 and 85 degrees with a basking spot of around 90 degrees; a regular nighttime temperature of about 75 degrees with at least one basking spot of 80 degrees; a water dish, changed daily, that is big enough for the ball python to soak in; one pre-killed mice every other week, fed to the ball python in a separated feeding enclosure to help your ball python become tame faster.

## Is your child ready for a reptile?

Because reptiles require careful handling and hygiene, experts recommend them for homes with children older than age 6. Reptiles are great pets for busy kids with lots of activities, since they do not need a lot of interaction to be happy and many do not even need daily feeding to thrive. The fact that many reptiles can go comfortably unattended for a day or two makes them a good choice for children whose activities might take them away from home on the occasional weekend.

Allergies to reptiles are incredibly rare. A bigger concern for reptile owners is the possibility of salmonella contamination, since reptile waste can contain this type of bacteria. It is important that children and parents clean their hands thoroughly after every reptile encounter and cage-cleaning session. If your child has trouble remembering to wash his or her hands or is prone to eye and face rubbing, he or she may not be ready for a pet reptile.

Does your child remember to put his or her toys away when playtime ends? Are all his or her game pieces fully intact in their boxes? Reptiles do best with children who are by nature neat and careful. It is important for children who have pet reptiles to remember to wash their hands after every play and cleaning session with their pet. Since reptiles love to slither out of their cages whenever they can, messy rooms are not a great idea for reptile owners — they offer too many hiding places for reptiles that have managed to make it out of their containers. Children who are neat and careful around their house and meticulous about doing their chores at home are also more likely to be able to follow through on the fairly stringent hygiene requirements of reptile ownership.

Parents should always take the lead in caring for your family's pet reptile, but your children can certainly join in the responsibility of caring for your new pet.

## Feeding

**Toddlers and preschoolers** can help keep your reptile's water container filled with a little adult help.

**Elementary-school kids** can also mark off days on a calendar to keep track of when feeding day is coming.

**Older kids around 12 and up** can feed reptiles under adult supervision, as well as the other activities described previously.

## Cleaning

**Toddlers and preschoolers** can help parents with cage cleaning.

**Elementary-school kids** can help with cage cleaning, as well as replacing liners or bedding with adult supervision.

**Older kids around 12 and up** can learn how to clean the cage and remove and change the cage liners by themselves.

## CASE STUDY: CONNECTING WITH CORN SNAKES

Parent: Andrea Clifford
Children: Benjamin and Cleo
Kansas City, Kansas

Andrea wasn't thinking about getting a pet, but Benjie had been having behavioral problems since his dad and mom got divorced a few years ago, and one of his therapists suggested he might do well with a pet. Cleo was only 2 at the time and Benjie was 6, so Andrea knew they needed a pet that did not need daily walks. Andrea is a nurse, so her hours can be crazy, and her sister — who lives with them and helps take care of Benjie and Cleo when Andrea is working — is in college, so the family's free time is limited.

One day, Andrea took Benjie to a pet store and let him look at all of the pets to see if there was one he liked. He thought the fish were cool but did not like the idea of cleaning an aquarium. He watched the little furry animals, like hamsters, for a while, but he did not seem excited until he saw the corn snake. When he saw that snake, his eyes just lit up, and he asked if he could hold it.

Andrea admits she was not a huge fan of snakes and did not really think a snake would make a good pet. She tried to steer Benjie toward some of the other pets, but he had set his heart on that corn snake. The store clerk explained to them what we would need — including a bag of frozen mice because there was no way Andrea was going to let Benjie feed his snake live mice — and they ended up taking home a corn snake.

Andrea was not sure at first, but it has been a great pet. Benjie is good about helping to keep the snake's cage clean, and she has even gotten used to the frozen mice in the freezer. The snake is actually very pretty, and Cleo loves to watch it sitting on its hot spot.

# Chapter 8

You Decided on Your Pet —
Now What?

Once you have made the decision to bring home a pet, the next question is where to find your pet. There are numerous options — at numerous price levels — for families shopping for their first pet. In this chapter, we will look at breeders, pet stores, animal shelters, rescue organizations, online resources, and word-of-mouth resources, and what you should know about each of these pet ownership options.

## Breeders

Breeders are animal specialists who mate specific animals in order to sell their offspring. Breeders — especially breeders of dogs — have gotten a bad reputation in recent years because of stories about inhumane breeding practices and mistreated animals. News stories about puppy mills (where dogs are bred over and over again to produce puppies for sale) and animals kept in tiny, unhygienic living quarters are common. However, there are reputable breeders out there and there are several reasons families might want to look to a breeder for their new pet.

For one, breeders specialize in specific breeds, so if your family has decided a Labrador retriever or an Abyssinian cat is the pet to have, a breeder can give you just that immediately. Finding the same animal through a shelter or rescue group could take much longer. Reputable breeders also work hard to ensure the health and happiness of their animal charges, so buying from an ethical breeder makes it more likely that you will end up with a healthy animal (some breeders even offer full return options for animals that are diagnosed with a genetic condition).

Reputable breeders are a wealth of information about the breed in which they specialize and can offer you insightful tips on how to train, care for, and play with your new pet. They are familiar enough with the animal they are selling to be able to tell you if the animal you are considering is especially playful or a little shy. Breeders can give you information about your pet's family history so you have an early warning about possible problems — such as arthritis or blindness — which may run in the breed. Breeders can be the best source for more unusual pets, such as birds or reptiles, which are rare in animal shelters and may not be available to buy at places other than a breeder.

Aside from the benefits a breeder can offer in your search for the perfect pet, buying from a breeder is not right for every family. For every reputable breeder, there are five unethical breeders who breed animals and keep track of paperwork irresponsibly. A bad breeder's puppies may have the right paperwork, but they are often sickly or bad-tempered because of their breeder's lack of knowledge. Finding a good breeder can be a challenge. Animals purchased from a breeder are more expensive than animals adopted or re-homed (adopted from another family), increasing the initial cost of your pet. Furthermore, if your family has decided on a breed of pet that is very rare or hard to find, you may not have a breeder in your area and may need to search long-distance.

## Pet breeds vs. Show breeds

Pet breeders who specialize in dogs or cats may classify their animals into two categories: Show breeds and pet breeds. Show breeds have been bred specifically for certain characteristics that make them ideal animals for competition. They may also make terrific pets but often cost more money than pet breeds, which are purebred animals that do not make the show cut because of marking differences or other characteristics. Either type can make a great pet.

## Finding a reputable breeder

Finding a good breeder can be one of the most challenging parts of buying your pet from a breeder. There are many places that advertise themselves as breeders but are actually little more than backyard pet mills, where animals are quickly bred in less-than-optimal conditions for the sole purpose of making money, or unknowledgeable owners with a couple of purebred pets. If you have decided to purchase your pet from a breeder, here are some places to look for one:

- **Area kennel clubs:** Look for a kennel club or breed-specific group in your area, and ask them to recommend a breeder.

- **Obedience-training courses:** If you have chosen a pet that can be trained, visit an obedience-training course to ask for breeder recommendations.

- **Veterinarians:** Your vet can help you find an ethical breeder (if you have not already found a vet who specializes in your particular pet, this is a good opportunity to find one).

- **Pet groomers:** Groomers who specialize in the pet you are planning to purchase can be a good source for finding reputable breeders.

- **Boarding kennels and pet daycare centers:** Check with your local pet care spots to see if they recommend any breeders.

- **Online:** The Internet is the first stop for many people looking for a pet, and it can be a good way to find basic information about breeders who specialize in the pet you are looking for. If you decide to look for a breeder online, be sure to ask for references — something any reputable breeder should be more than willing to provide — and check with local vets and groups to see what kind of feedback they can give you about the breeder from which your family is considering purchasing your first pet.

Classified ads in the newspaper are not usually the best resource for finding a reputable breeder, since anyone can advertise in the paper. If you decide to go this route looking for a breeder, highlight a few that you are considering and ask for feedback about the breeder at a couple of the sources mentioned above before you decide which breeder to visit.

When you visit a breeder, plan the first visit with the intention that you will not even visit with a pet; this allows you to get a feel for the breeder's work and ask your questions without the emotional attachment that it is so easy to form with a new pet. Buying a pet from a breeder is an investment, much like buying a washing machine or a new car, and just as you would research any big-ticket purchase, you should plan to invest thought and research in making your purchase. Buying a pet from a breeder can cost anywhere from $50 (for reptiles) to more than $3,000 (for certain kinds of birds, cats, and dogs). Use these criteria to evaluate your potential breeder:

*Does the breeder invite you over?* A breeder who resists having you visit his or her operation might have something to hide. If your breeder does not want you to see his or her premises, look for another breeder.

*What is the living area like?* A good rule of thumb is that you should not adopt a pet from a breeder if you would not be comfortable eating a meal or using the bathroom in his or her house.

*Where do the pets spend most of their time?* If the pets live mainly in the house, spending time with the family and each other, it is a good sign. If, however, the pets are kept outside or caged most of the time, socialization may be an issue, and your potential breeder might not be a good one.

*What does the owner say about the breed?* If he or she talks about the negatives of owning this particular breed of pet and answers your questions thoroughly and honestly, the breeder is likely to be a reputable one. A breeder who glosses over the negatives and cannot answer questions about the breed is cause for concern.

*How many litters does the breeder breed each year?* If it is more than one or two, you should proceed with caution. The same goes if the breeder says he or she breeds females more than three times in their lifetime. Have too many litters put stress on mother, as well as the other animals.

*How do the pets look?* Your breeder's pets should have shiny coats or skins, clear eyes, and no obvious discharge from the eyes or nose.

*Does the breeder have references?* Every reputable breeder should willingly provide references from other owners who have purchased one of his or her pets. Some may also offer references from their veterinarian.

*What is the purchase contract like?* Reputable breeders generally ask for right of first refusal if the time were to come when your family could no longer care for its pet and offer a health guarantee of at least one year. Be suspicious if you are dealing with a breeder who is not willing to include these guarantees.

*What health information does the breeder provide?* A good breeder will be able to talk to you about your pet's eye health history, joint health history (if applicable), and other health issues that may occur. Your pet should come with a thorough health examination when you purchase it.

## What About Age Limits?

Some breeders refuse to sell their pets to families with children younger than a certain age. Even if you think your 3-year-old is ready to handle a pet Lab, a breeder may decline to sell to you until your child reaches age 6 or older. Breeders invest time, energy, and money in breeding, and often are not willing to risk sending their pets to children who may not appreciate the care and gentleness needed for pet ownership.

If you have your heart set on purchasing a particular pet from a particular breeder with a strict age limit, you

may have to wait a few years until your child meets the breeder's age requirements. Keep in mind that animal shelters and pet stores may have less rigid requirements than many breeders do.

## Questions to ask and answer

Once you have decided on the right breeder, here are some questions you should ask before you purchase your new pet:

- Which of these pets do you think is right for our lifestyle? A breeder knows his or her individual animals well and can often pinpoint exactly which animal would be a good choice for a particular family. If you are bringing your children with you to help choose your pet, you might consider asking the breeder to choose two or three animals that might be a good fit for your family to consider so that you are not overwhelmed by too many choices.

- How much does the pet cost? Is that the same, or more or less than the other pets you have in the same breed? If it is more or less, why is the cost different?

- What health tests have been done on this pet? What health tests were done on the parents of this pet? A health history can really help guide new owners in their choice of a pet.

- Can I meet the parents? In terms of behavior, parents can offer a great deal of insight into how a pet will behave as an adult.

- What do you think are the biggest challenges with this type of animal? How do you recommend we handle them?

- What do you think are the biggest pleasures of this type of animal? How do you recommend we maximize them with our pet?

- What kind of food is the pet eating? How does it get its food? In general, it is best to keep your pet on the same food to which it is accustomed, including treats.

- What shots or other medical treatments has this pet had?

A good breeder will have some questions for your family, too. Be prepared to answer questions like the ones listed below — and keep in mind that breeders might be as particular about selling to you as you are about buying from them. Working through the sections in this book should have prepared you to answer all of these questions, as well as other questions the breeder might have about your family's readiness to take on a pet.

- Have you ever had this kind of pet before? What was your experience with this pet like?

- How many children do you have? How old are they?

- Do you live in a house or an apartment?

- Are you allowed to have a pet where you live? (some breeders may ask you for a signed letter from a landlord or community to indicate that you do in fact have permission to bring home the pet you want to purchase)

- Do you have other pets?

- Do you have a fenced-in yard?

- Where will you keep your pet's crate?

- Do you know the pet laws in your community?

- What kind of training are you planning for your new pet?

- Are you aware of the costs of owning this particular pet? Do you understand the needs of this particular pet?

- Who will your veterinarian be?

# Pet Stores

Pet shops tend to get a bad rap when it comes to selling pets, but a responsible, ethical pet shop can be a great resource for pet buyers, though these types of shops can be very hard to find. However, most pet stores — including big retail shops like PetSmart — offer in-store adoptions rather than pets for purchase because of the challenges of ethically selling pets, which require pets to have comfortable quarters and regular exercise that many retailers do not have the space, time, or staff to provide pets for sale. *To learn more about adopting an animal, check out the section on Animal Shelters later in this chapter.*

There are a few possible advantages to purchasing your pet from a pet shop. Some pet shops carry animals from local breeders, which can allow you to purchase a pet from a breeder without having to find a breeder yourself. If you are anxious to get your pet, most pet shops allow you to take home your pet as soon as you buy it, so there will not be a waiting period for your pet as you would have with many breeders and rescue groups. Pet shops also do not screen potential owners as carefully as breeders do, so if you have very small children, a pet shop may be a good place to shop for a pet instead of a breeder who might be reluctant to place in a family with very young children. Finally, because pet shops carry many different breeds of animals, you can test how your children interact with different breeds and different types of animals (most breeders specialize in one or two types of pet, so you need to know what you are looking for when you visit one).

However, there are a few things you need to consider before settling on a pet store as your place to purchase; in fact, it is best to consider a pet shop after you have explored other adoption options because there are a number of potential disadvantages to getting your animal from a pet shop. In most cases, the people selling you a pet at a pet store are not experts in that particular animal. They will not be able to give you very detailed information about how to best care for the animal you are purchasing. In the same way, buying a pet from a pet store means that you are unlikely to have access to information about the pet's parents and genetic proclivities. Some pet stores may be willing to put you in contact with the breeder or breeders they buy from, but keep in mind that very few reputable breeders deal with pet stores. You also have no guarantees of health or breed characteristics when you purchase an animal from a pet store. Even a pet that comes with official paperwork does not come with any guarantees; it is not even a guarantee that a pet is purebred.

Keep in mind that it is not difficult to get registration papers for most pets; a registration certificate may look official but only gives information about the pet's birth date and parents. The American Kennel Club — the gold standard for dog registration — for instance, requires only the parents of a dog be registered; not that they be healthy or meet any other criteria. Some pets, such as reptiles, may not have official registration or certification.

On top of health concerns, you do not have the opportunity to truly see how the animal has been socialized or to learn much about its upbringing. Many pet store animals are kept in cramped environments and poorly socialized, making them more likely to have health problems or be nervous or ill tempered. Finally, pet stores often inflate prices to breeder levels, even if their pets do not meet a breeder's standards, and are more expensive places to get a pet than adoption or rescue organizations.

# Buying an Animal From a Pet Store is Rescuing it, Right?

Once you know how animals are treated at pet stores, it can be tempting to consider purchasing your pet at a pet store to save it from such a miserable life. However, think twice before you do this. Though the instinct is a noble one, the truth is that you are perpetrating the system that allows unethical pet stores to exist. When you purchase an animal from a pet store that clearly treats animals in a way that is unacceptable, you are putting money in that owner's pocket and encouraging him or her to keep doing exactly what he or she is already doing. Another pet will immediately take the place of the one you have rescued, and it is impossible for one family to save every pet store pet that is suffering. In addition, the pet you purchase is

likely to have socialization issues that life with children may only exacerbate, and you may find yourself in the unhappy position of having to find a new home for the pet you "rescued." Purchasing or adopting a pet from a place that treats animals ethically is a better option, even though it can be hard to resist the pleas of the puppies in the window.

## Finding a proper pet store

A pet store that treats animals fairly and ethically is not easy to find, but look for these clues that will point you in the right direction:

*Where is the pet shop located?* As a general rule, pet shops in shopping centers like malls are not the best places to find animals because they are in places designed to encourage impulse purchases.

*What does the store sell?* A store with a thoughtful, thorough selection of supplies for the animal you are considering purchasing is likely to have animals that are treated better than a store with lots of animals and limited supplies. If you are buying fish, steer clear of pet stores that carry only one or two brands of fish food. If you are buying hamsters, avoid stores that carry only one variety of cage or shavings. A store that sells only one brand of products for a particular animal does not take into account that — much like people — pets are not a homogenous group who all automatically thrive with the same specific ingredients.

*Are the animals fully weaned?* Pet stores should not carry animals that are too young to be self-sufficient. In general, dogs and cats should be at least 8 weeks old, guinea pigs should be 4 weeks old, and other animals should exhibit characteristics of self-sufficiency. Birds, for instance, should be able to fly on their own. Stores that sell animals before they are ready to leave their parents are not likely to be ethical pet shops.

*What happens to the pets that are not sold?* The answer to this question can tell you a great deal about whether this particular store is a place where you want to purchase your family's first pet. Some stores will be intentionally vague about an animal's future to further motivate you to purchase a pet from them to save it from a worse fate. Most stores will tell you the truth: That a puppy who does not sell will have its price reduced until it does sell or may ultimately be given away or given to a shelter.

*How do the pets look?* Pet-shop pets should have shiny coats or skins, clear eyes and no obvious discharge from the eyes or nose.

*How are the pets housed?* If too many pets are cramped together in a small space, it is not a good sign since it indicates the animal is living is less-than-optimal conditions. Use the information in this book to make a mental note of how much room your pet of choice needs to be comfortable, and if you find the pet store's quarters too cramped, look for your new pet somewhere else.

*Where is the owner/manager?* It might be unreasonable to expect every pet shop employee to be passionate and informed about the pets for sale in the store, so ask to speak with the manager or owner. If he is on the premises and can talk intelligently about the pets for sale in his store, it is a good sign. If, however, the manager is never available or is unwilling or unable to provide information about the animals in his store, it would probably be wise to look elsewhere for your family's first pet.

## Questions to ask

If you decide to purchase your pet from a pet store, be sure to ask these questions before you buy:

- *Where do these pets come from?* Can I talk to the breeder? Can I visit him or her? A pet shop that does business with a reputable breeder should have no problem with a customer getting in touch with the breeder who supplies their pets.

- *Can I see the health records for this pet?* Can I see the health records for the other pets in this store? Because many illnesses are contagious and pet store quarters can be close, if one animal in a store gets sick, others are likely to follow suit. If your potential pet has been exposed to an illness, it is important for you to know about it before making your purchase.

- *What kind of health guarantees do you offer?* Pet stores may offer anything from no guarantees to a lifetime guarantee, but be sure you understand the terms of the agreement completely. For instance, a pet store may allow you to return your dog in three years when it develops hip problems and replace it with a new puppy, but for a family that has grown to love its pet, returning it to a pet store that will likely put it so sleep is not an acceptable option. A guarantee showing that your pet comes from a family without medical issues is better insurance against future problems than a return policy.

- *What kind of food is the pet eating?* How does it get its food? In general, it is best to keep your pet on the same food to which it is accustomed, including treats.

- *What shots or other medical treatments has this pet had?* Can I get a copy of the veterinary report?

## Animal Shelters

Animal shelters, including places like the ASPCA and the national or regional humane society, can be one of the best resources for families looking for a new pet. Some pet stores offer shelter-style, in-store pet adoptions, which follow the same principles as a shelter adoption. Not only can adoption be one of the most affordable ways to bring home a pet, it is also a way to provide a home for an animal that truly needs one.

Many experts suggest beginning your pet hunt at an animal shelter, since the animals that live there are eagerly waiting for homes. You are giving a home to an animal that needs one. Most animals in shelters have found their way there because previous owners could not take care of them properly, and they are grateful to have a second chance at a happy home. While animals in shelters are mixed breed, about 25 percent of all the animals in animal shelters are purebreds. Because mixed breeds are typically less expensive than purebreds, adopting an animal is much more affordable than purchasing one. You also have the option to adopt older animals rather than just puppies and kittens. Though young animals are cute and playful, older ones often make better pets for families. For example, most shelter dogs are between 6 months and 2 years old.

Shelters get new animals all the time, so there are usually a variety of animals to choose from. If you want a particular animal that is not in the shelter, you can ask to be notified or put on a waiting list for when an animal like the one you are looking for comes into the shelter. Because there is a constant stream of animals, you can spend time with several different types and breeds of animal to see which one really suits your family best. Furthermore, many animals at a shelter come with detailed health history. Some even come with health information about parents and grandparents. Volunteers and staff at shelters also spend a lot of time with the animals at their shelter and can tell you about their personalities and quirks. Most shelter pets also have the opportunity to learn basic manners (sit, stay, come) from the volunteers and staff, and living around so many different animals can teach them tolerance — an important quality in a pet that will be living in a house with a child.

Though there are a number of reasons to consider an animal shelter as your first stop when looking for your family's first pet, there are a few possible disadvantages that you should keep in mind. Shelters may have a limited selection, so if you are looking for a particular breed of dog or an exotic animal, you may have to wait for your shelter to receive one to adopt. Some shelters also do not carry animals other than cats or dogs, so you might have to look elsewhere for other types of pets. Finally, some animals end up in shelters because they have been abused or neglected. These pets may have behavior problems that even love and training cannot repair.

## Locating an A+ animal shelter

You may be surprised by how many animal shelters are actually in your area. Shelters are usually organized by local government or by local humane societies, and even small towns usually have at least one animal shelter. In big cities, you may have a dozen different shelter options to choose from. A good place to find a list of shelters in your area is Petfinder (**www.petfinder.com/shelters. html**), where you can enter your zip code to see a list of shelters near you. Some pet supply stores, including PetSmart and PetCo, also have regular shelter days where they help facilitate adoptions. As a rule, it is wise to visit a prospective shelter without your children for an initial visit because it can be hard for children to understand that they might not be bringing home that cute kitten or sweet parakeet they got to play with at the shelter. Here are some ways to find the right shelter for your family's first pet:

*What kind of application do you have to fill out?* A good shelter is likely to ask you for references and information about your family and finances to make sure you are able to adopt one of their pets.

*Do you feel welcome?* Good shelters love to have potential adopters come in and should greet you warmly and answer your questions. If the shelter is very busy when you come in and the volunteers and employees do not have time to focus on you, you should still feel welcome when you walk in.

*How do the staffers treat the pets in the shelter?* If the staff members are kind and talk to the animals and play with them as you go through the shelter, it is a good sign. Even better: If the staffers tend to know most or many of the animals in the shelter by name, it suggests that the animals there get a great deal of loving attention.

*What kind of space do the animals have?* Most shelters have to keep animals in cages or crates during part of the day, but good ones have play areas for the animals to get in needed recreation time whenever possible.

## Questions to ask

When you find the shelter where you want to adopt, ask these questions as your family is choosing its perfect pet:

- Do you have an animal here that seems like a good fit for our family?
- How much does it cost to adopt the kind of pet I want? Is there a price difference if the pet has already been neutered or spayed?
- What kind of supplies do you provide for the pet?
- What kind of food is the pet eating? How does it get its food?

- What shots or other medical treatments has this pet had?
- How did this animal get here?

Sharing information about your family and what you are looking for in your first pet can help your adoption counselor pinpoint a particular pet or pets that might work well with your family. Because they spend a lot of time with animals that come into the shelter, adoption counselors may have noticed a particularly well-behaved cat or a dog that seems especially gentle with children. Animals who end up in animal shelters may have been given up by owners who can longer care for them, or they may have been rescued from pet breeding mills, picked up off the street, brought from local shelters or surrendered by kennels or veterinarians' offices where they were abandoned. Finally, you will want to know what kind of diet (food and treats) the animal is currently on in order to keep it consistent when you bring it home. The pet might not enjoy a new brand of food and switching its diet can upset the animal's stomach.

## Rescue Groups

Rescue groups — also called adoption placement groups — are like shelters in that they take in animals who have been abandoned or mistreated, but unlike shelters, they specialize in a specific breed or type of animal. Also unlike shelters, rescue groups rarely have brick-and-mortar locations, relying on volunteer fostering to care for pets in search of a home. If you are looking for a specific animal and unable to find a breeder you want to work with or can afford, a rescue group can be a good alternative. The group can tell you what it knows about a particular animal's history and parentage.

Just like shelters, rescue groups can be an excellent starting point for families looking for their first pet. Because rescue groups specialize in particular animals or breeds, you can get a purebred or unusual animal more easily than through a shelter or pet store. You are also giving a home to an animal that truly needs one. Most animals that end up in rescue groups are there because they were not taken care of properly, and they can be grateful to have a second chance at a happy home. Because volunteers are responsible for fostering the rescue animals instead of having them in a shelter, the animals adopted out by rescue groups are more likely to be socialized than animals in a shelter. Spending time in homes also makes it easier for rescue organizations to pinpoint any behaviors or characteristics of a particular animal that might make it hard for that animal to cope with life in a family environment. They also have the opportunity to see firsthand which animals make good family pets. Adopting a pet from a rescue group is often less expensive than purchasing a pet from a breeder or a pet store.

While it does feel good rescuing an animal in need, adopting from a rescue group also comes with a fair share of certain challenges. Some rescue groups may not adopt to families with children younger than a certain age under any circumstances. If your child is younger than the required age, the rescue group will not give a pet to your family. Rescue groups are also more geographically sparse than shelters, and there may not be one in your area, meaning you might have to go through a long-distance adoption to bring home a pet from a rescue organization.

Because rescue groups are volunteer ventures for the most part, it may be difficult to get quick responses to your questions. There also may be a long waiting list for the pet you want, and rescue organizations often require a lengthy application and approval process, which may include home visits as well as references. Adopting a pet from a rescue group is more expensive than adopting a pet from an animal shelter, since the cost often includes veterinary costs and other expenses of the animal's care during its fostering. Finally, some animals end up in rescue organizations because they have been abused or neglected. These pets may have behavior problems that even a lot of love and proper training cannot repair.

## Researching your rescue group

Finding a rescue group is not difficult, but it is unusual to find a group with a physical location near you. Most rescue groups rely on volunteers to foster rescued animals until they are ready to go to their adoptive homes, so there is usually no central location for you to visit and observe. If you can visit a home that is sheltering a pet in your area, that would be ideal, but it is not always possible. You can use directories such as **www.allaboutdogsandcats. com/Dogs/BreedRescue.html** or **www.akc.org/breeds/rescue. cfm** to help you in your search for the rescue group that is closest to you. Here are some things to look for as you are getting to know a rescue group:

*What kind of application do you have to fill out?* A rescue group is likely to ask for extensive interviews, as well as references and information about your family and finances to make sure you are a good adoptee for one of their pets.

*Do you feel welcome?* Not all rescue organizations are helpful and friendly, though those organizations are the exception rather than the rule. Still, if a group is not welcoming, it is unlikely that your reception will warm up with time so it might be best to look for your pet elsewhere.

*How organized does the rescue group seem?* Since most rescue groups are staffed entirely by volunteers; meaning you cannot necessarily expect the same level of responsiveness and customer service you would get from someone who makes animal adoption their full-time job. These are grass roots organizations and could take weeks for somebody to get back to after an initial inquiry about a pet. But if you find your responses from the group are nonexistent rather than just slow, or if you cannot get reasonably quick answers to simple questions, you might be better searching for a place to find your pet that is better able to help you with your search.

## How to Find a Rescue Group

If you are looking for a rescue group for a particular breed, start your search here:

- **Check with your local animal shelter:** Shelters and rescue groups often work hand-in-hand to find homes for animals. Shelters may seek out rescue groups to help find homes for animals that shelters do not have room for, such as fish or snakes.

- **Look online:** Though groups seem to come and go, research rescue groups for your specific breed on different search engines. These

will give you a good place to start investigations.

- **Local clubs and organizations:** Kennel, breed, and enthusiast clubs for the particular breed or animal you want to adopt can often point you toward rescue groups for that breed.

## Questions to ask and answer

When you are adopting a pet from a rescue group, it is a good idea to ask the same kinds of questions you would ask when adopting your pet from an animal shelter. Because rescue group volunteers are often passionate owners of that particular breed or type of pet themselves, they can also be a good source of information about the pet you are adopting.

- *Do you know of an animal in your organization that seems like a good fit for our family?* Sharing information about your family and what you are looking for in your first pet can help your adoption counselor pinpoint a particular pet or pets that might work well with your families. A group's leader can canvass the current pet foster parents to see if there is one exhibiting the kind of characteristics that would be right for your family.

- *How much does it cost to adopt the kind of pet I want?* Is there a price difference to adopt a male versus a female pet? Is there a price difference if the pet has already been neutered or spayed?

- *What kind of food is the pet eating?* How does it get its food? In general, it is best to keep your pet on the same food to which it is accustomed, including treats.

- *What shots or other medical treatments has this pet had?*

- *How did this animal get here?* Animals who end up in rescue groups come from the same places shelter animals do, and in some cases — especially for specific breeds or unusual animals — shelters may work with rescue groups so that they can accept pets that need special care for surrender and then pass them onto a rescue group to be fostered and connected with a new home.

- *What do you think are the biggest challenges with this type of animal?* How do you recommend we handle them?

- *What do you think are the biggest pleasures of this type of animal?* How do you recommend we maximize them with our pet?

Like breeders, rescue groups will have numerous questions for you to answer before they even put you on their list for adoption. Be prepared to answer questions like the ones listed below — and keep in mind that rescue groups are very particular about the families where they place their animals. Like some breeders, some rescue groups may flat out refuse to consider placing a pet in families with children younger than a certain age, and if you are committed to getting a pet from one of these organizations and have children below the age limit, you may have to wait until your child is older to adopt. Working through the sections in this book should have prepared you to answer all of these questions, as well as other questions the rescue group's adoption or placement counselor might have about your family's readiness to take on a pet.

- Have you ever had this kind of pet before? What was your experience with this pet like?

- How many children do you have? How old are they?

- Do you live in a house or an apartment?

- Are you allowed to have a pet where you live? Some rescue groups may ask you for a signed letter from a landlord or community to indicate that you do in fact have permission to bring home the pet you want to purchase, just as breeders do.

- Do you have other pets?

- Do you have a fenced-in yard?

- Where will you keep your pet's crate or container?

- Do you know the pet laws in your community?

- What kind if training are you planning for your new pet?

- Are you aware of the costs of owning this particular pet? Do you understand the needs of this particular pet?

- Who will your veterinarian be?

## Thinking Outside the Crate

Though the places outlines here are probably the most common places that people find pets, they are far from the only places. Though less reliable than the places above, you may have luck finding your dream pet through one of these sources:

### Classified ads

Though we would not recommend finding a breeder through classified ads alone (see the previous section on breeders for details), the classifieds in your local community newspaper and online can be a good way to find animals looking for a new home. Because classifieds can be very much hit-or-miss — you may find a loving owner who needs to find a beloved pet a new living space or a stranger who breeds hundreds of puppies in pens in his or her backyard — it is a good idea to thoroughly investigate before making a commitment to a pet you find in the classified advertisements. Engage in an exploratory phone conversation, using the questions in the breeder section above, and if you feel satisfied with the answers, ask to have the animal examined by an independent veterinarian. If you are comfortable with the results of the conversation and examination, visit the animal and move on from there.

## Word of mouth

Most people hear about pets needing new homes fairly regularly from neighbors and colleagues. Your coworker might have found a pet dog sniffing around her back porch that will not go away, or your traveling neighbor might be looking for a new home for her pet bird. If you put out the word that you are looking for a particular pet, you may find more offers of pets than you can handle. Just be sure to thoroughly investigate any pet before you bring it home.

## Online

Many shelters and rescue groups participate in online databases that allow you to search for specific animals online. You can look for particular breeds or characteristics, animals in your area or animals of a certain age. As with any place that sells animals or places them for adoption, you will want to thoroughly screen the person or organization offering the pet using some of the questions we outlined above, but the Internet can be an excellent starter resource for families looking for a pet. Some sites to try include:

- **Petfinder.com:** Lets you search through pets available for adoption using a variety of filters, including location, breed and age. Most of the available animals are dogs and cats, but you can also find birds and small animals, including reptiles. There are no fish listed on the Petfinder.com site.

- **Adoptapet.com:** Connects you with shelters and pets awaiting adoption in your area. Again, dogs and cats are the most common animals on the site, but they also list birds, small animals, and fish looking for homes.

- **Craigslist.org (look under the pets section in your city or region):** Offers a hit-or-miss listing of pets available for sale, adoption, or re-homing in your neck of the woods. Ads can be placed by owners with no vetting required, so exercise caution when you are pet hunting on Craigslist. Use common sense, and always check out breeders and re-homers (who may be breeders in disguise) before you purchase a pet or pay a re-homing fee.

- **Facebook marketplace:** Lists pets for sale by Facebook users in the "Everything Else" section. You can search for pets for sale in your area or through your network of friends and associates. If you are dealing with someone you do not know, use caution and common sense when purchasing a pet.

# Chapter 9

Pet Care 101

O nce you have decided to bring a new pet home, you will probably want to rush out the door to find your perfect animal and bring it home. Bringing home a pet will be an exciting day for your family and probably become a special family memory, so make an effort to do it right.

## Preparing for Your Pet

Give yourself at least a week to prepare your home for a new pet. This may seem like a long time, but you will be busy — perhaps busier than you would expect. This time is also a good opportunity to start your children on the right track for pet ownership by teaching them how to be responsible for a pet.

While it is true that you can bring home the essential gear listed for each of the pets in the previous chapters at the same time that you finalize the adoption or purchase of your pet, it is a good idea to have your pet's necessities in place before you bring it home.

Your family will want to spend those first minutes with your new pet in your own home without worrying about whether you need to set something up or figure out how to put something together. Take advantage of the pet-free days to familiarize yourself with your pet's gear and supplies: Learn how to securely fasten and unfasten crates and cages, find a cup or dish to measure food, and figure out a good location for litter boxes, feeding bowls, cages, and other equipment. You will also want to put up doggy gates to block areas that will be off-limits if you have a cage-free pet, such as the stairs, your office, or your baby's room. Being prepared for your new pet will make bringing home your pet a stress-free experience. Here are some things you should do before your new pet comes home with you:

**Find a veterinarian:** This is fairly easy to do for common pets, such as dogs and cats, but you may have to do some calling to find a vet who treats unusual animals if you have decided to bring home a bearded dragon lizard or canary. It is important for your family to find a vet for your new pet even before you need one for a couple of reasons. First, you will want to make an appointment for your new pet as soon as you bring it home to be sure that it has a clean bill of health. Second, just as you probably found a pediatrician while you were still pregnant with your child, you should be prepared with a responsible care giver for your pet so that if your pet does become sick, you do not have to waste time trying to track down a veterinarian.

**Set up your pet environment:** Again, compare your situation to bringing home a new baby: Just as you would not wait until after coming home from the hospital with your newborn to put together a crib, you do not want to have to try to figure out how to hook up your aquarium's water pump or your bird cage's water bottle in the chaos of your pet's first few minutes at home. Completely put together any equipment that needs to be assembled, take the tags off chew toys and other playthings, start your aquarium running, set up and fill up your litter box, and take care of any other advance set-up you can manage before your pet comes home.

**Find a pet store:** It makes sense to wait until you have gotten your animal home to stock up on food — you may want to use the same food the breeder or shelter has been using, or you may want to test different foods to see which kind best suits your pet — but you should buy a few basics to ensure you can get through the first couple of days. It is also smart to find a go-to shop for pet supplies. If your new pet is a dog or cat, you can probably get by with shopping for your basic pet needs when you do your grocery shopping and plan excursions to specialty pet stores when you need to; but if you have chosen a more unusual pet, you may need to work harder to track down the supplies you need. Even if you plan to order most of your pet supplies online, you will need a local store that you can rely on if you have an emergency.

**Create a First-aid Kit:** Just as it is a smart idea to keep antibiotic spray and soft bandages on hand when you are a parent, it is a good idea to be prepared for pet emergencies, too. Post your new veterinarian's number in a prominent spot where you can easily find it, and set up a kit with scissors, surgical tape, and gauze, as well as styptic powder and antibiotic ointment. To be truly ready to cope with emergencies, keep your kit in a small travel carrier or cage so that you can quickly transport your pet to the vet or animal hospital. Take advantage of your first veterinarian visit with your pet to talk about common ailments for your pet and how to treat them at home. Keep in mind that what is a safe home remedy for one type of pet might not be safe for another. Your vet might recommend giving Pepto-Bismol® to a dog with an upset stomach, but the same remedy could be fatal to your cat. It is always a good idea to check with your vet before trying a remedy you have heard about or spotted on the internet.

**Pet-proof your home**: Since you have children, this should be a familiar process. Basically, your task is to protect anything that could cause damage to your pet or that your pet could seriously damage. This means putting all potentially toxic products, such as cleaning or car care supplies, into safe storage, protecting electrical cords and outlets, and removing expensive rugs and furnishings in areas where your pet will be. These basic pet-proofing strategies are a good idea for most pets. Some pets, such as birds, have special preparation needs. *Check the chapter on your particular pet for safety hazards specific to it.*

## Saving Grace

If your perfect pet is out of your budget now, start your pet preparations by saving for your dream pet. Let your children decorate a container — a clean spaghetti jar or empty coffee canister works well — with pictures or stickers of their hoped-for pet. As you set aside money for your pet, store it in the container. Or, make a chart for the wall with the needed amount of money and fill it in with markers or crayons as you move incrementally closer to your pet savings goal. For families who

really want a pet, this can be good way to work together toward your desired result.

## How to find a veterinarian

It is always a good idea to check with a vet first when you have questions about your pet's health. Just like your pediatrician's office can give you advice about taking care of your new baby, a vet's office is a great resource for learning how to take the best care of your family's new pet. Most vets will not charge you for a quick phone call, and you can be sure you are getting the right information for your pet. Of course, you could also consult a pet store or other resource, if you choose. If you are new to owning a pet, you may be clueless about finding the right animal doctor. Here are some resources to help you find a pet health care provider for your new pet.

- Ask for referrals. Family, friends, and coworkers can all be potential resources for finding a good veterinarian.

- Ask when you adopt or purchase. Shelters, breeders, shops, and rescue groups are usually familiar with local pet health care and can recommend vets who specialize in your particular pet.

- Call your state's Veterinary Medical Association and ask them to identify vets in your area who treat your pet of choice.

- Ask for recommendations at your local pet supply store.

- Check your phone book. You will have to make a call to find out if a vet treats your particular pet, but you can find an extensive list of vets in your phonebook's Yellow Pages.

Be sure to confirm that your vet will, in fact, treat your particular pet. Though most vets treat cats and dogs, you may need to find a specialist if you have chosen a bird or reptile for your pet. Keep in mind if you have chosen a very unusual pet, you may not have a vet in your area who is experienced treating that pet. Be prepared to travel if necessary. It is also a good idea to find contact information and directions for your area's emergency pet treatment facility or animal hospital, just in case you ever run into an emergency with your pet.

## Naming Your Pet

One of the more fun parts of bringing a new member home is getting to choose its name. Everyone in your family will want to weigh in on your new pet's name, but making a decision may be harder than you think. If you are looking for inspiration, consider one of these sources. Whatever name you decide on, try to choose it during your first two weeks with your pet so that it will quickly learn to respond.

Capri after places where you have made happy memories together.

**Your favorite books:** Get inspired by characters from your favorite books. Your children may be excited to name their new dog after one of their favorite fictional characters, like Hagrid, Bella or Caspian, or you might get inspired by one of your favorite stories and vote to name your cat Mr. Darcy, Ender Wiggin, or Ford Prefect.

**Places you love:** Place names lend themselves well to pet names. Consider naming your new hamster duo Bleecker and Cornelia after a favorite New York City intersection, or name your dog Arizona, Juneau, or

**Sports heroes:** The names of famous athletes can also make good pet names. Christen your fish in honor of your favorite tennis or hockey players, or name your new dog after your all-time favorite mascot — Gator might be a perfect fit for your new Boxer.

**Celebrities:** You could name your new pet after one of your favorite celebrities. You will be in good company if you do: Actress Jennifer Garner named her pet dog Martha Stewart after the lifestyle maven, and Eva Longoria called her pet dog Oprah.

# When You Bring Your Pet Home

When the big day comes, everything has been signed, sealed, and delivered, you will need to be ready to bring your pet home with you.

Even if your pet will not spend much time in a crate or cage, you will need some way to get your pet safely home. Letting a new pet ride unconfined in your car is not a good idea, since pets can get nervous and could cause an accident by jumping onto an unsuspecting driver. If you already have a carrier or cage for your new pet, you are good to go. If you do not have one, ask around to see if you can borrow a container or pick up an inexpensive one that you can resell later if you want to. Since most pets need to travel occasionally, even if it is just to and from the veterinarian, it is not a bad idea to keep a small, travel carrier around.

Your children are probably thrilled about the prospect of bringing home your family's new pet, but consider leaving them at home for the actual pickup. Even under the best circumstances, car trips are stressful for pets, and children can unintentionally up stress levels with their (understandable) excitement. If you do bring children with you to pick up your pet, talk to them before you leave about how important it is for them to be calm and quiet in the car. Let an adult be responsible for holding the new pet on your drive — little fingers may find it hard to resist poking in the cage, which could result in unnecessary biting or scratching.

## The first night

A new home can be a wonderful thing for many pets, but the first few hours in a new home can be a little nerve-wracking.

Your home is a new place, full of unfamiliar people, sounds, and smells, so do not be surprised if your pet reacts by hiding. Small animals might cower in their cage's hiding places, and cats and dogs might squeeze behind a couch or under a bed. It is a good idea to explain this behavioral tendency to your children before your new pet comes home so that they are not surprised by their new pet's behavior.

When you bring your animal home, relocate it to its permanent cage if it is going to live in a cage or open the carrier to let it out if it is not a caged animal. If your pet is already in its cage, put the cage in its predetermined location and leave the door open once the area is secure. Make sure your new pet has food and water in its cage or that it knows where its food and water is located. Then — and this is the hardest part for many children — leave the pet alone for a few minutes. Let your pet become familiar with its new surroundings; before long, it will be coming over to check you out.

Do not get alarmed, but your pet may seem skittish or nervous for a few days. Your pet may have accidents, urinate more frequently than normal, or have diarrhea. Your pet may eat or drink more or less than normal (obviously, your idea of normal will be based on what you have learned about your pet through reading and asking questions since you will not have experience to base your idea on). If this continues for more than a couple of days, check with your new vet, but it is normal for animals to experience a period of adjustment in their new home.

## Microchips

Microchips — tiny, computerized chips that contain tracking and contact information for your pet — are becoming an increasingly popular option for pet owners whose pets might stray outdoors. If your pet gets lost and returned to a shelter or vet, a quick scan will reveal your pet's owners and get your pet back home quickly. Though the idea of a microchip can seem a little Robo-Pet when you first hear it, a microchip can be a useful tool for some pet owners. If you are thinking about a microchip, here are some things you should know:

1. Getting a microchip implanted feels like getting a shot. Because the chip is so tiny — tiny enough to fit on the tip of a hypodermic needle, in fact — the implant process feels just like a routine shot to your pet. Granted, it may not like getting a shot, but it will not cause any physical harm or long-lasting discomfort for your pet.

2. Chips are not just for dogs. There are several different types of microchips designed with different types of animals in mind, so it is worth checking with your vet to see which type might be right for your pet.

3. Expect to pay a one-time fee between $20 and $50 for your pet's microchip. Vets and animal shelters set their prices for microchips individually so your costs may vary.

4. Just getting a microchip is not enough. You have got to activate your microchip — usually through a computer Web site — for it to be effective. If you move or change phone numbers, you will need to update your contact informa-

tion with the microchip registry. You may have to pay a one-time registration fee or an annual maintenance fee or both to list your pet's information in the registry.

5.  One microchip will probably last the life of your pet. According to the Humane Society, the annual lifespan of a microchip is about 25 years.

6.  A microchip does not replace your pet's collar and identification tags.

## Do Not Forget Your ID

Even the best-taken-care-of pets can get lost, and making sure your pet has identification is an important part of being a responsible pet owner. Dogs and cats can wear a collar with your name and contact information on it. Consider getting an identification band for your bird to wear on its leg. Smaller pets are more likely to get lost inside your house than outside it, but if you are taking your guinea pig out for regular walks, you will need to make sure it has a collar and tag, too.

## Making a Home for Your Pet

Whatever kind of pet your family has chosen, it is a good idea to take it for a checkup with your chosen veterinarian within a few days of bringing it home. This is a good idea for several reasons. First of all, it is your opportunity to make sure you have not gotten a pet with serious underlying health issues. Even pets that come with health certifications — and certainly those that do not come with those guarantees — can have health problems that might not have been diagnosed. An early vet visit is also a good opportunity for your new vet to get to meet your pet. After that, your pet's health needs will vary depending on what kind of pet you have chosen. Here is a pet-by-pet breakdown of what to expect for your pet, including how to protect your pet's health and how to make your pet comfortable in its new home:

## Dogs

Your pet dog will quickly feel like part of the family, and you will have to keep it healthy using many of the same tools you use to keep the rest of your family healthy.

### Vet Visits

Your dog will need an annual checkup and visits to stay on your vet's vaccination schedule. As you get to know your dog, you will become familiar with its behavior — how it acts when waking up in the morning, when it needs to go outside, when it likes to play, and how often it eats will all become part of your daily schedule. Dogs cannot tell you when they feel sick, but their behavior can tell you if you are paying attention. If you notice dramatic changes in your dog's behavior patterns that you cannot explain by something happening around you — for instance, a dog's sleeping patterns changing during a neighbor's noisy house renovation — call the vet. Dogs also exhibit some of the same symptoms people do when they are sick, including runny noses, runny waste, and general listlessness.

## Potential Problems

Dogs are prime targets for fleas and ticks, tiny pests that burrow beneath your dog's coat to bite and suck the sensitive skin below. Depending on your pet, your vet may recommend a pest-repelling medication, shampoo, collar, or combination of methods to fight fleas and ticks in your pet dog.

If you live in a part of the country where Lyme disease — a condition caused when a person or animal is bitten by an infected tick — is common, your vet may recommend specific measures you should use to safeguard your dog's health, such as Lyme disease vaccinations, collars, or topical treatments with insecticides. However, vaccinations are somewhat controversial: The human version of the vaccine was taken off the market because of its limited effectiveness and associated risk for developing a serious — and untreatable — form of Lyme disease in some people who were vaccinated. Follow your vet's recommendations to keep your pet healthy.

Dogs are also prone to heartworms, a serious health problem that can usually be prevented by medication. There are several different brands of heartworm and flea medications, including Frontline, Comfortis, Advantage, Heartgard Plus, K9 Advantix, Sentinel, and Interceptor. Ask your vet for a recommendation and dosage guidelines, then shop around to find the best price on the brand he or she recommends.

Your pet dog also needs plenty of activity to help it maintain a healthy weight; like you, your dog will start to put on pounds if it spends too much time sitting around and not staying active. If your dog gains too much weight, it could develop joint problems, shortness of breath, or cardiovascular disease.

## TRaining

If you bring home a pet dog, one of your first goals as a pet owner should be to teach your dog to follow simple commands. Dogs who are not trained to follow simple commands rarely do well with families. If you do not have any experience with dogs, consider taking a dog obedience class with your new pet — some humane societies offer low- or no-cost obedience training sessions for pet owners. Training a dog is not difficult, but if you have never done it before, you may need help getting started. In general, training works best when you reward your dog for good behavior and give him positive reinforcement. It also helps to get your dog comfortable around other people by taking it places like the park and the pet store with your family. If it is socialized, it is less likely to bite or scratch strangers for no reason. Keep in mind that even a dog that is good with children should not be left alone with young children for long stretches of time. Training a dog can be a family project, and while there are plenty of books and classes that can help you through the specifics, here are a few general guidelines to get you started on the right track:

Focus on praising good behavior rather than punishing bad behavior: When your puppy follows through on a desired behavior — whether it is standing calmly at your side when you stop to chat with someone at the park or using the bathroom outside — be generous praising its good behavior, petting it, offering treats, and telling it what a good job it did. Your dog will want more praise and will try to repeat the behaviors that earned it.

Discourage bad behaviors by walking away: Some behaviors, like biting, could have serious consequences and you cannot just ignore them. A practical, non-punitive way to end biting, jumping, and other problem behaviors is to say "Playtime's over" and walk away when they happen (obviously your puppy might jump or bite at times other than playtime, but rambunctious behavior is more likely to occur when you are having fun). Your dog will learn to associate biting and other bad behaviors with the end of playtime and will be less likely to do things that make the fun end.

Work with your puppy to train him: If you are trying to teach your puppy to walk on a leash, let it check out the leash and give it free rein now and then to test its limits. If you are teaching your puppy to come when you call, gradually build up its understanding by offering treats and starting with a few steps before you build up to longer distances.

Your child can get involved with your dog's training, too. Though parents should take the primary responsibility for dog training, children can help reinforce commands by playing games with your dog. Try playing a puppy version of musical chairs to teach your dog to come when called: Gather the family in a circle with your dog in the middle, and take turns saying "Come" or your dog's name (you can also use this game to practice sitting, speaking, or lying down). Reward your dog with a treat and praise when he goes to the right person. Be sure your child understands that only one person at a time can call your dog, or you might end up with one confused puppy.

To teach your dog to walk calmly on a leash with your child, try a game where your child walks your dog on its leash up a flight of stairs, one step at a time. When your child says "stop" or "heel," both of them should freeze, and your dog should not move again until your child says "walk." If it pulls on the leash, they go back to the bottom and start over. When they reach the top, give your dog a treat and praise both the dog and your child for training for their good work.

## Cats

Cats adapt quickly to new surroundings, though they may be skittish for a few days while they become familiar with the rhythm and sounds of their new home.

### Vet Visits

Like dogs, cats need annual vet visits for vaccinations and general health screening, as well as visits when their health is below par. Cats have many of the same problems with fleas and ticks that dogs do, and vets use the same combination of pest-repellent medication, cleaner, and collars to protect cats from fleas and ticks. As with a dog, you will quickly learn to spot the signs of illness in your cat when it deviates from the routine you have become accustomed to: If it eats more or less, has accidents outside its litter box, acts listless or hyper, it is a good idea to call your vet to find out what is going on.

### Litter Box

Cleaning the litter box can be a hassle, but it is part of being a responsible cat owner. It is actually not too difficult to train a cat to use the litter box. Because cats tend to be fastidious about their waste, if you show them the litter box a few times, they will be inclined to use it. Be careful, though, because once your cat has become accustomed to a particular kind of litter, it might not handle a change well. Some cats will stop using their litter boxes — and start using less-than-ideal places like your bedroom as their urinals — after a litter change.

## Training

A cat is probably not ever going to fetch the newspaper for you, but you can teach your cat not to scratch your baby or the furniture. A water spray bottle is a safe, effective tool for controlling your cat and can easily be purchased from stores like Walmart or Target. Cats do not like to be squirted with water, but since it does not hurt them, using water to correct behavior can be an effective method of steering your cat toward better behavior.

## Birds

Birds are sensitive, intelligent creatures that will delight your family with their pretty ways. You need to be a responsible bird owner by knowing how to make your new bird stay healthy and feel right at home.

## Vet Visits

The APCA recommends bird owners take their birds for an annual vet visit every year since vets weigh birds at every visit to make sure they stay healthy. Though it may be hard for you to notice a weight change in your tiny bird's body, significant changes in weight can be one of the best clues for recognizing a serious health problem in a pet bird. Birds have delicate immune systems and can become dangerously ill very quickly, so it is important to call the vet if you notice signs of sickness. Keep an eye out for behaviors like fluffing feathers, sitting on the bottom of the cage instead of on a perch, changes in the appearance of your bird's droppings, sneezing or coughing, wheezing or crusty residue around the eyes or beak, and contact your vet if you spot any of these symptoms.

## Training

Birds learn fast, but they need time to learn how to trust you and your family. To build trust with your bird, open the bird's cage and put your hand in without grabbing or handling your bird. Give your bird a chance to sniff and explore your hand, and wait until it is comfortable with you to introduce him to the next member of your family. Birds can be trained to do all kinds of tricks once they are comfortable with you: The reward method, in which you give your pet a treat such as popcorn or a sunflower seed, when it succeeds, works well. If you have chosen a talking bird, use persistent repetition and a cheerful voice to repeat one word or phrase over and over to your bird until it repeats it. When it does, offer it a treat and start on a new word. Keep in mind that it can take many months and even years of patience to teach a bird to talk, and some birds are naturally more talkative than others.

## Fish

Fish rely on their environments for all their needs, so making sure they are in a healthy environment is a fish owner's No. 1 concern.

## Vet Visits

Most fish do not need annual vet visits, since fish do not get vaccinations or need regular medication to stay healthy. But fish do need to see a vet if they become sick. Take note of changes in the appearance of your fish that could signal a problem, such as color changes, swollen bellies, spotting or discolorations, or damaged tails. If you spot any of these symptoms, call the vet. After you have owned your fish for a while, you may be able to purchase over-the-counter remedies for many common fish illnesses, but you should get any symptom checked out by the vet until you are confident you recognize the symptom and the condition it reflects. If a fish does become sick, you will need to remove him to a separate tank as he recuperates so he does not get your other fish sick, since most fish diseases are highly contagious. Common contagious fish illnesses include bacterial infections, like dropsy and fin rot; fungal infections such as ichthyosporidium (also known as white spot); and parasitic infections, including flukes, anchor worm and nematode.

## Tank Care

It cannot be overemphasized the importance of keeping your fish tank clean and healthy for your fish. Know how much space different kinds of fish need to thrive, and do not pack more fish than can live comfortably into an aquarium together. Follow the procedures for keeping your tank clean that the tank manufacturer recommended. Though different types of fish might have similar characteristics, you might find that your fish that is supposed to get along with other fish is actually quite territorial. That is because fish — much like people — have both individual and species characteristics.

# Water, Water Everywhere

Every pet needs access to fresh, clean water. Making sure your pet has clean water every day — whether it is swimming in it or drinking it — is essential to maintaining your pet's good health.

## Feeding

Overfeeding fish is a common problem for new owners. As a general rule of thumb, your fish need as much food as they can consume over about a 2-minute period. If they get more food than they need, the leftover food will decompose in the tank, causing cloudy water and contamination that can make fish sick.

## Small Rodents

Even small rodents need plenty of care to keep its energy level high. Pet-proofing your house is an essential part of taking care of your small pet, but there are other things to keep in mind, too.

## Vet Visits

If you are going to have two small pets of the opposite sex, it is a good idea to have them neutered and spayed unless you want lots of little furry babies running around — hamsters can have as many as 16 babies in one litter, though they average five to ten babies. Otherwise, some people recommend annual visits for small rodents and others suggest visits on an as-needed basis, so it is up to your family which choice feels right. Still, it is a good idea to schedule an initial healthy pet visit to make sure your small pet is healthy and to provide a starting weight and behavior record for future visits. Use the same symptoms you would use for other pets to spot signs of illness in your small pet: crusty or water eyes, listless behavior, changes in eating or bathroom habits, and coughing or wheezing can all point to health problems in a small pet.

### Training

Since your small pet will spend most of its time in a cage or container, you want to be sure it associates its container with safety and comfort rather than with punishment. Especially in your early days as a small pet owner, give your pet time to adjust to its cage and make its own way inside rather than forcing it. Also, do not get drawn into a game of chase when it is cage time, or your pet will get the idea that going into its cage is a game, which is a bad precedent to set.

## What Every Pet Needs

Now that you are a pet owner, your pet is a part of your family and taking care of your pet's health and happiness is part of your job. Whether you have adopted a frisky kitten, a well-manned, middle-aged dog, or a tank of beautiful fish, there are certain things every pet needs to live a happy life.

### Food

Pets do best with a regular feeding schedule, and most pets get accustomed to a particular time of day they are fed and a particular kind of food. If you change its usual diet, your pet will need time to make an adjustment. You may add a little of the new food to your pet's previous food, gradually increasing the amount of new food until your pet is only getting the new food. If you are changing foods because your pet has had a bad reaction to its previous food, your only option is to be patient as your pet adjusts and continue to offer the new food. In general, it is a good idea to avoid giving "people food" to any pet, since food that is right for people to eat can make animals sick. Your pet also needs a designated food spot, where it knows it can find its food bowl and water.

## Shelter

Even an animal that spends most of his time outside needs a shelter to protect him from storms, wind, cold, and the elements. For small animals that spend most of their time in cages or containers, it is important to make sure their shelter is as comfortable and spacious as they require. Bigger animals may not have a crate or container, which means your house, a doghouse, or even a covered porch might be their shelter. Be sure your pet has a space where it feels safe and is protected from the elements and possibly predators.

## Bathroom

Your pet does not need indoor plumbing, but it does need a spot to use the bathroom. If you take your dog for bathroom walks, remember that cleaning up after your pet is part of the responsibility of dog ownership — your apartment complex most likely has rules in place requiring you to clean up after your pet — and bring your pooper-scooper and plastic bag with you. Other animals need to have their waste areas regularly cleaned: Whether it is a litter box or a cage liner, your pet's bathroom should be cleaned once a day or as needed. Just think about how you would hate to use a dirty bathroom, and appreciate your pet's need for a clean space to eliminate its waste.

## Exercise

Every animal needs to move to play healthy, so it is important to make sure your pet has plenty of space and plenty of opportunity to be active. This may mean making sure you have the right number of fish in your tank or that your hamster's cage is the recommended size, or it may mean running every night with your pet dog. One of the benefits of pet ownership is that it can help you to be more active, too, so encourage your family to actively embrace your pet's need to move by getting their heart rate up.

## End-of-life Care

It is sad to think about, but since most pets have shorter life spans than humans, you will probably face the issue of a dying pet someday. It is incredibly difficult to lose an animal you have loved to death, but you can make decisions that will help your animal die with dignity and without suffering. There is no one right way to deal with the death of a pet, but your veterinarian can guide you through the available options when the day comes so that you can make the right choice for your pet. Depending on your pet's condition, you may choose to care for your pet at home, caring for its needs and following your veterinarian's recommendations for pain relief, or euthanasia, if your pet's suffering is extreme and you want it to have a peaceful death. These can be difficult decisions to make, and you might want to seek help from a counselor or therapist in making them.

## Love

The most important thing every pet needs is love. All other responsibilities of pet ownership aside, pets that are loved by their owners thrive. The exchange of genuine affection is one of the best parts of pet ownership, so embrace it — and enjoy it.

## CASE STUDY: LEARNING FROM A VET

Jonathan Reed, D.V.M.
Newnan, Georgia

As a vet, Jonathan meets a lot of new pet owners. Most pet owners have good intentions and want to forge a healthy relationship with their pet, but sometimes they do not know how to do that. Here are some things he wants pet owners to know in order to have a better relationship with your animal:

- It is OK to call the vet when you have a question. Jonathan does not know if people think they are going to have to pay every time they call or if they are just embarrassed not to know something, but there have been many times where he has had to treat an animal for something that could have been prevented if that animal's owner had just called. Think of your vet like your doctor: Sometimes you call with a question that does not require a visit, and that is not a bad thing. Do not make a call to your vet your last resort.

- Have a backup vet. Jonathan has a one-man operation, so he always makes sure his patients know the number of the local animal hospital and of a fellow vet's practice in case they run into trouble at a time when he is unavailable.

- Pay attention to your pet. You need to know what your pet's waste normally looks like, its usual gait, its usual eating habits, and its normal behavior so that you know when something is abnormal.

- Keep a first-aid kit so you can give your dog emergency or routine treatment at home. Ask your vet how to put one together at one of your regular visits: Jonathan is always so happy when a patient's owner asks him about putting together a first aid kit because it shows foresight.

• Think about getting pet insurance. You do not need it for every pet, but if you have a pet with a long lifespan who may be genetically predispositioned to hip problems or cancer, pet insurance can help pay for treatments that would otherwise be very expensive for families.

# Chapter 10

Challenges

O nce you have gotten through the first few bumpy days and settled into a routine, your new pet will quickly become part of the family. You will have plenty of new responsibilities that will quickly become familiar parts of your daily and weekly to-do list, and you will also find that you get to enjoy many of the happy benefits of pet ownership. You will enjoy watching your pet and your child get to know each other, and you will want to keep a camera handy to capture the first game of fetch, the first time your pet falls asleep on your child's lap, and all the milestones your child experiences as he or she learns to care for his or her new pet. Of course, once you have become pet owners and gotten comfortably familiar with your new pet, you can still run into situations that throw you for a loop, from moving to bringing home new babies. This chapter will take you through some of the most common challenges pet owners face and give you the information you need to handle them.

## Hot Stuff

Every summer, parents are horrified by news stories about people who leave their children alone in a hot car, a situation that can lead to dehydration, illness, and death. Your pet, whether it is a lizard or a Lab, is just as susceptible to the dangers of heat, and you should never leave your pet alone in the car when it is hot outside, not even for a few minutes. Your pet could become seriously ill or even die. Even if your pet is OK, your action could lead a well-meaning observer to report you for animal cruelty.

## What if You Move?

Moving to a new home can be just as stressful for your pet as it is for the rest of your family, so it is important to help your pet make the transition as smoothly as possible.

Before your intended move date, make sure your pet will be welcome in your new home. You will need to check with your new landlord, apartment complex or homeowners' association, as well as checking the relevant portions of your new town or city ordinances for laws about pet ownership. If there are any issues regarding your pet's legality — for instance, if your dog weighs more than your new condo's listed maximum pet weight or if your apartment complex prohibits reptile ownership — it is usually possible to get an exception made for your pet. Doing so takes time, however, so if you do run into a problem, you should get started on the process of pleading your case as quickly as possible. If your landlord agrees to allow your pet, be sure to get his permission in writing as part of your lease so that there will be no question about the pet policy later. Do not wait until the last minute to verify your pet's status in your new home, or you could end up having to move without your pet.

Just as you pack your children's favorite toys and linens in an "open first" box for your new home, pack up your pet's essential supplies, including its bedding, feeding supplies, toys, and medical records so that you can quickly unpack them and set them up in your new home. Your new pet will want to get adjusted to its new home just as much as you want to get adjusted.

Update your phone number on your pet's ID tag a few days before your move, and if you have a microchip, update your contact information with the microchip registry, too. With all the activity of moving day, it is easy for a pet to slip out of a door and get outside, so it is a good idea to have your current contact information on your pet's collar. Plus, nothing would be more frustrating than losing a pet only to have the incorrect contact information on its tag.

Consider getting your pet out of the house on the day of your move while you are packing up and moving out of your old home; your pet will know that you are going somewhere, and all of the commotion could be confusing and stressful for your pet. Look for a kennel for a short-time boarding session or ask a friend to pet sit at his or her place so that you do not have to worry about keeping an eye on your pet while you are trying to coordinate your move. If you want to keep your pet at home, keep it in a secure room where it can wait safe and confined for the loading to end.

If you are moving a small pet, reptile, or bird that spends most of its time in a cage, you will want to keep your animal secure in its cage during your move. To do this, remove any food and water as well as any items that could get dislodged and injure or frighten your pet during your travels — such as toys or perches — from the cage before covering the cage with a clean, light-weight cloth. You should also keep your animal's cage covered during the move.

Keep in mind that animals, especially reptiles and small animals, are very sensitive to changes in temperature. Try to keep their temperature as consistent as possible by keeping their crates or cages away from drafts and open doors and not keeping them in direct sunlight. Also, never leave animals alone in a house with the power turned out overnight or for a long period of time, since they could be exposed to potentially fatal extremes of heat or cold.

Keep your pet contained — in its cage or in a safe area — until you have had a chance to get settled in a little bit. Obviously, you will not want to leave your pet locked up until you unpack that last box of childhood mementoes three years from now, but do give yourself a chance to get the basics organized and set out a few familiar things before you let your pet loose in your new space. Depending on how comfortable you feel, you might want to wait an hour or longer before letting your pet out.

As you are unpacking, look for ways to keep things familiar. If your aquarium was near a large mirror in your old home, try a similar position in your new home. If your cat is used to having her food in the laundry room, try to keep its food in the laundry in your new home. You certainly will not be able to duplicate your pet's old environment and you should not stress yourself out trying to do so, but it is a good idea to make things as familiar as you can.

Introduce your pet to your new surroundings just as you did on the day it joined your family. Fish will probably adjust fairly quickly, but it will help other pets to get out of their cages for a few minutes exploring the new space or letting your dog or cat sniff around their new home. Let your pet sit on your lap or near you, and gently stroke it, talking comfortingly to it. As it becomes interested in checking out its new surroundings, let it. If its food and water containers or litter box are set up, show your pet where to find them. If you have a dog, take it on a walk around the yard and new neighborhood. If you have small pets, keep a close eye on them since you are in a new place where you do not know every nook and cranny, and you do not want to have to do a hamster hunt on your first night.

Be reassuring and patient. Just as it might take you a few weeks to get the hang of your new kitchen or a few nights for your children to be comfortable sleeping in their new room, expect your pet to have similar adjustment hurdles to overcome.

# What if You Have a New Baby?

A new baby is a big adjustment for the whole family, including your pet. If your pet was around when your other children were young, it probably knows a little about babies, but if your children were older when your pet joined the family, the prospect of bringing home a baby can be stressful. After all, babies are fragile and easily injured, and once your new baby comes home, you will have a lot less time for your pet — not to mention a lot less time for sleep and showering. It is possible to have a new baby and a happy pet at the same time, but you are probably going to have to put in some effort to make it happen.

Get your pet ready for a new baby before it arrives by introducing your pet to the sounds and smells that will come with a baby. Animals rely heavily on sensory input to make sense of their surroundings, and smell and sound play an important role in how comfortable they are at home. Among the many other changes a new baby brings are significant changes in the smells and sounds of your home. Start by stocking up on supplies you will use to care for your baby, such as diapers, baby soap, and baby-safe laundry detergent, and let them become a part of your home's smells gradually. Watch programs or movies that feature baby sounds, like crying and cooing.

Invite a friend with a baby over to visit so that your pet can get a sense of what having a baby in the house is like. Your pet can learn that there are special rules for babies — you are not allowed to jump on them, for instance — and that they get lots of special attention from the other people in the house. If your pet has never been around a baby before, you should be extra vigilant about watching your pet while the baby is in your house. As you set up your baby's crib and other supplies, discourage your pet from spending time in the baby's space. Let your pet check out the baby's space thoroughly, but then block it off and let your pet know that this is not their space.

If you will be making big changes at home — transforming an office where your pet spends a lot of time into a nursery or moving a lot of furniture around — take care of these changes several months before your due date so that your pet has an opportunity to adjust before your baby comes home. You do not need to be worrying about making sure the pet feels comfortable in your home when you have a new baby at home.

Once you bring the baby home, you will want to be careful to watch your behavior toward your pet when you are caring for the new baby. Of course you need to help your pet understand the rules of being near the baby, but if you are always snapping at your pet or saying "no" when you are holding the baby or in the baby's room, your pet is likely to associate the baby with bad feelings. Make a point of smiling at your pet or petting it when you are holding or feeding the baby. Tell your baby what your pet is up to: Say things like "Comet is being such a good boy sitting here looking at you have your snack. I bet Comet cannot wait until you are big enough to play with."

Your other children will be adjusting to the newest member of your family, too, so if their age and maturity warrant it, the advent of a new baby makes a good opportunity to increase their pet care responsibilities. Consider letting an older child take over responsibility of the evening feedings, for instance, with parental supervision, and encourage your older kids to spend time with their pet when you are caring for the new baby. Your older children and your pets will both benefit.

Do your best to keep your pet's familiar routine in place. If you know something will have to change, switching from a morning walk to an evening one for instance, try to make the change as gradual as possible and start preparing your pet for it in advance.

Make sure your pet still gets special one-on-one time with you and other family members. Parents are always pressed for time, and a new baby can make it even harder to find spare moments, but it is important for your pet's happiness to ensure that it gets individual attention every day, even if it is just for a few minutes.

## CASE STUDY: ANOTHER BABY ON BOARD

Parents: Kristin and Michael Warren
Children: Haley and David
Jacksonville, Florida

Michael had a 12-year-old daughter, Haley, when he married Kristin in 2006. The family adopted a beautiful Siamese cat named Blue shortly after Kristin and Michael got married, and Blue became an integral part of the family. Haley spent part of her time with Kristin and Michael and part of her time with her mom, and Blue became the family baby. Kristin, Michael, and Haley all spoiled her with treats and attention, and Blue just ate it up. But in 2008, Kristin got pregnant, and she, Michael, and Haley had to prepare their furry baby for a real baby.

At first, it was a real challenge. Blue was not used to anything being off limits and tried to take naps in the baby's new crib and bassinet. When the baby came home, Blue jumped up beside little David and tried to climb on his face — the same way she often climbed on Haley's face when she was watching television on the couch. Kristin had new-mom jitters and started to panic every time she saw Blue coming into the room; she would grab baby David and shut herself up with him in the bedroom with the door closed so that Blue could not come in. Then, Blue started to knock things off shelves and urinate on the furniture. Kristin, feeling hopeless, thought they had to get rid of the cat if they wanted to keep the baby safe.

Haley came to stay for a month that summer, and though she was excited about her new little brother, she also spent plenty of time with Blue, petting her and playing with her while her stepmom and dad were busy with the new baby. Michael commented that Blue seemed to have shaped up with Haley in the house, but Blue went back to her bad behavior when Haley went back to her mom's. Kristin tried to figure out what had been different when Haley was there, and she realized that the big difference had been that Blue had someone to pay attention to her. She started spending a few minutes with Blue every morning while she had her coffee, and she began to notice Blue's behavior improve. Once Blue was better behaved, Kristin started spending less time locked up in the bedroom and more time in the family areas of the house. Blue became more careful around David, and Kristin started to feel comfortable letting Blue sit beside her while she fed David or burped him. Once Kristin and Michael stopped ignoring Blue, she became a sweet furry sibling to her new little brother.

# What if Your Pet has Problem Behavior?

You can do all the right due diligence, — choose your pet responsibly, and do your best to make your pet comfortable in your new home — but sometimes a pet comes with already established behavior problems from either personality traits or how it was raised when young. Though there are signs you can look for (*see the chapters on the different types of pets for tips on personality characteristics to look for when you are choosing your pet*) sometimes it is not clear that a pet's behavior is a problem until you have had a chance to get to know it. Here are some of the most common animal behavior problems and how to cope with them.

## Aggression

Most pets show their aggression by hissing or growling, baring their teeth, or snapping or biting. When you have children, these behaviors can be especially scary. It is usually possible for an adult to regain control of an aggressive animal but much harder for a child to do the same thing.

If you can, try to determine what is causing your pet's aggressive behavior. Does your pet get aggressive when someone goes near its food or a certain possession? Is your pet aggressive when something scares it or startles it? Is your pet territorial? Make observations, and ask your vet to evaluate your pet for any medical problems that could contribute to its aggressive behavior.

Once you have eliminated medical problems, ask your vet to recommend an animal behavior specialist who can help you work with your aggressive pet to train it. As you are working on a solution, take precautions to protect your children and other people from your pet's aggressive behavior. Keep your pet out of potentially volatile situations, consider a muzzle when it's out in public and confinement when it is at home and limit its contact with your children. Above all, don't respond to your dog's aggressive behavior with punishment or aggression of your own since this is likely to escalate the situation.

## Phobias

Phobias are irrational fears that manifest in panicked behavior that can include running, jumping, barking, and biting. Dogs are the animals most likely to develop phobias, which are often caused by loud noises, such as thunderstorms or fireworks.

If your pet has a phobia, it is usually fairly easy to help your pet overcome its fear with a combination of medication and behavior therapy. Ask your vet about prescribing a short course of medication to help your pet get over its phobia, and work with an animal behavior specialist to coach your pet to cope with its phobia in a healthier way.

Though most pets need professional help to overcome their phobias, there are a few things you can do at home to help your pet. If your dog's phobia is noise-related — such as a fear of fireworks or thunderstorms — playing music that contains similar sounds and gradually increasing the volume can help your pet become accustomed to the noise. In fact, music in general may have a calming effect on frightened pets. If you know what is causing your dog's phobia, you could also try a little reverse psychology: For instance, if your dog panics at the annual fireworks demonstrations, make the Fourth of July a special day for your dog with treats and its favorite activities.

## Obsessive grooming

Occasionally, a pet will become so obsessed with grooming itself that it will rub and lick its skin until it creates a bald spot and damage their skin, sometimes causing sores on the surface of the skin, commonly referred to as hot spots.

If your pet has become an obsessive in its grooming habits, ask your vet to recommend a short-term medication (there are prescription and over-the-counter medications available at your local pet store) while you work with an animal behavior specialist on behavior modification techniques to retrain your pet's grooming habits to a less destructive form. In the meantime, you might want to give your pet a cone, coat, claw covers or other protective covering so that it cannot hurt itself while grooming.

## If All Else Fails

Sometimes, your pet simply does not work as part of your family. Even though you have tried your hardest to integrate your pet into your family, it just might not fit. Perhaps you thought you understood how much work a pet would be, but after two months of extra shifts at work and no time off, you have realized that your pet is not being properly cared for. Perhaps your dog constantly snaps at your children, even after you have done your best to help it adjust, talked to your vet, and tried obedience training. Perhaps you have had no choice but to move to a new place where your pet reptile simply is not allowed.

Re-homing your pet, giving it to a new family, is obviously a last resort, but if you truly cannot keep your pet, it is your responsibility to do your best to find it a new permanent home. If you are in a position where you have to give up your pet, there are a few tips to help it find a new home. First, have your pet spayed or neutered. Most people prefer to adopt pets that have already been spayed or neutered, so if your pet has not been fixed now is the time to do it. You should also take your pet to the vet to get a clean bill of health. Get a copy of your pet's health records while you are there so that you can give a complete health record to your pet's new owners.

Be sure to describe your pet. Make a list of your pet's characteristics, including personality and behavior. Some people are looking for a "high-energy, very playful puppy" while others want a "laid back, calm cat that sleeps a lot." Be specific and be honest as you come up with a description for your pet so that people can easily tell whether your pet is one they would be interested in. If your pet is anxious or high-strung, say so. You may think that you are doing your pet a favor by fudging on its personality flaws to find it a new home, but you do not want your pet's new owners trying to re-home it six months down the road for the very same reasons you're trying to find it a new home now. Honesty increases the chances that you pet will find its forever home. Be specific about your pet's physical appearance, too: Do not just describe your pet as cute. Photos are a great addition. In general, use the same strategies you use to take pictures of your children to get a good picture of your pet. Get down to your pet's level, take pictures with the light behind you and snap lots of photos to get one or two really good ones. People are more inclined to purchase a pet when they know what they are looking at.

Put together a flier or e-mail with your pictures and description. Post your flier at work, at the gym, at the supermarket, at your child's karate studio, and every other high-traffic place you can think of. E-mail the information to your family and friends and ask them to pass on the word, too. You can also post your information on a site like Petfinder.com or Craigslist.org. You could also ask for a small fee to reduce the risk that you will be giving your pet up to someone who might want to use it for inappropriate purposes, like illegal dog fighting or research laboratories. This can help you even out some of the costs of giving your pet away, or you could donate the fee to a local animal shelter or rescue group that can help other pets who have been given up find a home.

Be sure to interview anyone who is interested in your pet in person. If someone gives off a bad vibe or you are nervous about sending your pet home with them, wait until you find an adopter you feel good about.

If you cannot find a suitable adoptive home for your pet, look for a shelter, rescue group, or animal welfare organization. Be aware that many shelters require a fee if you give up your pet — for instance, the Progressive Animal Welfare Society (PAWS) in the Pacific Northwest requires a $50 donation for an adult cat — but these fees can be waived if the alternative is that you would have to abandon your pet (think about how much money your pet costs each month, and it is easy to see why some groups require people giving up their pets to give a donation). Ideally, look for a no-kill shelter that does not euthanize pets that have failed to find homes within a set period of time. It is important to remember that giving a pet to a shelter is not the same thing as finding it a new home. Though some pets do find new homes through shelters, the fact is that many do not, and by giving your animal to a shelter, you are creating the possibility that your pet may spend the rest of its life in a shelter environment. That is why it is so important to exhaust all your resources in finding a new home for your pet before resorting to giving it to a shelter or rescue group.

## What to ask a potential adopter

You should have specific questions for the person who is going to adopt your family's pet. When you took on the responsibility of your pet, you agreed to look out for your pet's welfare, which means making sure it ends up with a responsible, loving home — and not in a puppy mill or other unloving situation. Invite potential adopters to meet you and your pet in a neutral place, and spend some time asking questions to get to know potential owners. Here are some to get you started:

- What is your name, address, and phone number? (Ask to see the person's driver's license to verify his identity.)

- Do you already have animals? If so, how many? What kinds? How will you introduce the new pet to your current pets?

- Have you owned pets before? What is your experience with pet ownership like?

- Can I get your veterinarian's contact information so I can check with him as a reference? (If a person says he or she has pets but does not have a vet, this is a red flag. Of course, a person who does not have a pet might not have a vet, so you can ask for a personal reference instead.)

- Where will the pet spend most of its time? Make sure your pet will kept in a safe, comfortable environment; for instance, you would not want to re-home your indoor cat to a family who plan to keep it outdoors.

- What kind of exercise will the pet get?

- Can I bring the pet to your place for a home visit? This is a good way to get a sense of what your pet's life will be like in its potential new home.

CASE STUDY: PLENTY FULL
WITH A POMERANIAN

Parents: Holly and Jake Arnold
Child: Caroline
Chattanooga, Tennessee

The Arnolds' friends Linda and Nick were gung-ho about getting a pet dog, and they went all out and bought an expensive purebred Pomeranian that really was adorable. However, they had no idea what they were getting into. They could not believe how much attention and energy a puppy required. Within about two weeks, they had gotten over how cute the dog was and decided to get rid of it. They asked Holly if she wanted it one day when they ran into each other at the playground, and her daughter Caroline absolutely fell in love with the little puppy. He was adorable, but Holly did not want to make the same mistake Nick and Linda made, so she said they would have to think about it.

Jake, Holly, and Caroline did a lot of research on Pomeranians. Caroline was 11 at the time, and she wanted the dog very much, so Jake and Holly told her she could try to convince them. She found all these facts about Pomeranians to show why one would really be a great pet for their family. She did all the research about what they would have to do to care for the dog and came up with a plan for how she would help with all the chores. It was pretty convincing — and the puppy was pretty cute.

So the Arnolds adopted Linda and Nick's Pomeranian puppy. Caroline changed his name to Schroeder after the Peanuts character, and they all loved him, but the first few weeks were hard. It was a lot like having a new baby. They had to teach him how to let them know that he needed to use the bathroom, get him into a routine, and teach him how not to jump and scratch. Holly could understand how having a puppy was so hard and why Nick and Linda did not want to have to deal with it. There were plenty of nights where she did not want to take Schroeder out for a walk or where she just stood in the living room and looked at all the spots on the carpet he had made and wanted to scream.

In the end, the Arnolds are glad Nick and Linda made a bad choice because they love Schroeder and could not imagine their family without him, but it breaks Holly's heart to think about sweet animals like Schroeder ending up in shelters or on the streets because their owners do not bother to understand what having a pet really involves.

# Chapter 11

Living With Your New Pet

As your family grows, you will face new adventures in pet ownership. Perhaps you will load up the car for a big family road trip with your pet along for the ride.

Just as your children grow into activities as they get older, classes or activities (dog Frisbee, pet massage, or tricks and show classes) may stimulate your pet. You might be so happy with your addition to the family that you decide to get another pet. As your pet gets older, you will build a collection of terrific memories.

## Traveling With Your Pet

Though you might hire a pet sitter or board your pet for some types of travel, other times you will want to bring your pet with you when you leave town. Though it requires some preparation, traveling with your pet does not have to be complicated or stressful. Whether you are going by plane, train or automobile, if you are taking your pet on a trip with you, there are certain things you should do before you hit the road.

Ask your vet for a recommendation or look online for emergency animal hospitals in the area where you will be traveling. Of course it is unlikely that anything will happen to your pet, but on the off chance that you do need to seek medical attention for your pet while you are traveling, you will not have to waste time trying to find an animal hospital if you have already done the legwork.

Be aware that not all public transportation systems permit pets to travel. If you are planning to use public transportation, such a buses or subways, during your trip, check to be sure pets are allowed on board. If they are not, you will have to come up with a Plan B, and it will be much easier to do that when you are not in a bus station with tired kids and a restless pet ready to reach their destination.

Book a hotel or accommodation that is pet friendly, and let them know you have brought your pet with you. Do not try to "hide" your pet in a place that does not welcome pets, or you could end up with hefty fines. If you leave your pet alone in your hotel room, be sure to put the "Do Not Disturb" sign on the door and let the front desk know that you have left your pet. Do not leave your pet alone in a hotel room for long periods of time. If you are doing something where your pet is not welcome or allowed, you will need to find a local kennel or pet sitter to take care of your pet while you are unavailable.

It may be hard to find the food and grooming supplies your pet is accustomed to when you are out of town, so it is a good idea to pack them, especially the food your pet is used to eating. Also pack your pet's usual sleeping materials. Having familiar food and items in an unfamiliar situation will make your pet more comfortable. If you are camping or spending time outdoors, keep in mind that your pet may be exposed to animals that could bite or otherwise injure it. Make sure your pet's rabies and other vaccinations are up to date to avoid any infections. Check with your vet before your trip to be sure your pet does not need any special medications or vaccinations before your trip.

If your pet hates change and does not do well with unfamiliar situations, consider finding a kennel or pet sitter and letting your pet stay home during your trip. Of course you will miss each other, but your pet may be happier to stay in a familiar place.

## Planes

If you have to fly with your pet, most pets are required to travel in the plane's cargo area. Some airlines allow pets in the cabin as long as they meet breed and weight requirement, but you should check with your airline on its pet policy before making your reservations. Regardless, all pets must be in a kennel or cage for air travel. Many pets get nervous when they are flying, so ask your vet

Need a Pet Sitter?

If you need a pet sitter to care for your pet and you do not have a friend or neighbor who can help you, visit the National Association of Professional Pet Sitters to search for pet sitters by ZIP codes.

about a tranquilizer to keep your pet calm during the flight. It is important to check with your vet about sedatives because high altitude can affect the potency of some sedatives, and you could cause medical problems for your pet if you try to medicate it without your vet's input and recommendations.

Follow up with the airline immediately after booking your flight to confirm that you are traveling with your pet. Because airlines allow only a limited number of pets on a flight and reserve the right to refuse travel to pets if there are already enough pets on board, confirm your pet's flight arrangements well ahead of time in order to avoid any problems when you get to the airport. It is also a good idea to reconfirm your pet's flight the day before your plane is scheduled to take off.

Some airlines require a certification from your vet indicating that your pet's vaccinations are current. It is not a bad idea to have this certification even if your airline does not require it in case you end up with a zealous ticket agent or miss a flight and have to be rescheduled on another airline's flight where the vaccination certificate is required. Keep your pet's vaccination certificate with your other travel documents so that it is easy to pull out when someone asks to see it.

Make sure your pet's collar and travel container are clearly labeled with your name, address and phone number. Since you are traveling, it is smart to include your cell phone number as well as your home phone number so that someone can reach you if necessary. You might also include the number of the place you will be staying at your destination to be on the safe side.

Never let your pet out of its travel container on the plane or in the airport. In a busy airport, a loose pet is an invitation for trouble. Keep your pet and your fellow travelers safe by keeping your pet in its travel crate, cage, or kennel.

If your pet uses a leash, be sure to stash it in a purse or carry-on bag so that it is handy when you leave the airport.

For more information on flying and traveling with your pets, consult one of these Web sites:

- LuxuryPaw.com
- DogFriendly.com
- PetsWelcome.com
- BringFido.com
- PetsOnTheGo.com
- TripsWithPets.com

## Cars

Road trips are often the easiest option for families with children and pets since they give you the freedom to stop for snacks, playtime, and bathroom breaks when the need arises.

If you are traveling by car, secure your pet just as you do your children. A sudden stop could send an unsecured pet flying across the car and could potentially cause serious injury to it and to you. Most animals should travel in a cage or kennel, but some dogs can ride on the seat. If your pet is traveling in a cage or kennel, use a seat belt or other method to firmly attach it in place. If your dog is traveling on the seat, invest in seat belt attachment that will hold it in place; you can find special pet seat belt attachments at pet stores and some discount stores.

Some pets have a tendency to get carsick on long trips. Check with your vet about medication for motion sickness and be sure you understand dosage instructions before you set off. You should never give you pet "people" medication or any medication your vet has not recommended or prescribed.

Never leave your pet unattended in your car, even for a few minutes. If you need to, take turns going in to the bathroom or send one person to pick up food for everyone and eat at a rest stop instead of in a restaurant or on the road. Your pet will appreciate the break and might enjoy the fresh air and open space.

Be sure to give your pet plenty of water while you are traveling, and try to keep its feeding schedule as consistent as possible.

## Pets Welcome

When you are traveling, it is fairly easy to check with a hotel in advance to make arrangements for your pet, but if you are on a road trip without definite spots, finding a place to stay for you and your pet can be tricky. Check out Petswelcome.com (**www.petswelcome. com**) to find a comprehensive list of chain hotels' pet policies so you know what hotels have pet friendly policies. Call the chain's 1-800 number to confirm that you understand their most current rules, and you

can safely stop with your pet at any of the hotel's locations without worrying about whether your pet will be welcome.

# Fun Things to Do with Your Pet

Once the initial thrill of pet ownership has settled down to contented happiness, you can keep things exciting by implementing some of these fun ideas. The more you get to know your pet, the more you will start to know the things it loves to do and the more activities you will find to do together. In the meantime, these ideas should get you started.

- Visit a dog park, pet play zone, or pet play date where your pet can interact with other pets and explore new toys and play equipment.

- Play fetch. Many animals other than dogs get excited about a fun game of fetch. Try tossing different objects to your pet to see what it decides to bring back.

- Create an obstacle course for your pet. This can be especially fun for small animals like hamsters or reptiles, but dogs, cats, and birds may enjoy it, too. Even fish enjoy having new items added to their tank.

- Make your own toys. You can always buy new toys, and it can also be a fun family activity to try to come up with toys that your pet will love.

- Set up play dates for your pet just as you do your children, and give your pet a chance to interact with other animals while you hang out with their owners.

- Go on a field trip with your pet. This obviously works best with animals that will walk on a leash, but many animals respond well to new locations, like farms, forests, and even rivers.

- Have a birthday party for your pet every year, complete with a homemade, pet-pleasing cake (you can find numerous pet snack recipes online), decorations and presents.

- Outfit your pet in a fabulous ensemble. Unless you have a pet fish, there is a kitschy costume out there for your pet. If your pet likes dressing up, the possibilities are endless. If not, well, at least you have some cute photos.

- Have a family portrait taken that includes your pet and use it for your annual holiday cards.

- Make plaster prints for everyone in the family using a kit from a craft shop. Let your pet add its paw to your children's handprints.

- Volunteer together. Many hospices welcome visits from pets and families; you can find opportunities in your area at **volunteermatch.org**.

- Have a dance party. Almost all animals enjoy music, and a rowdy, playful singing-and-dancing session will lift your pet's spirits as much as yours.

## CASE STUDY: PLANNING YOUR POOCH'S TRAVEL

Parents: Louise and Derek Callaghan
Children: Sasha and Meredith
St. Louis, Missouri

In 2007, the Callaghans moved from a little town in northeast Florida for St. Louis because of Derek's job. At the time, Sasha was 7 and Meredith was 5. They have had Lucky, their pet poodle, since Meredith was born, so there was no question that she would be making the trip with them, but it was much more complicated than they thought it would be. At first they planned to fly, but then they found out Lucky was over the weight limit to ride on the plane with them, and she would have to ride in the baggage compartment instead. They knew that lots of dogs do it all the time and are fine, but Louise could not stand the thought of Lucky having to do it — it was like imagining one of the girls having to travel in a suitcase.

So Derek and Louise decided to drive instead, which turned out to be a good idea because it allowed them to take more stuff with them and their movers ended up arriving a week later than they were scheduled, but that is another story.

Derek and Louise grabbed fast food and took it to rest stops so the girls and Lucky could eat and stretch their legs and use the bathroom. Between the kids and the dog, they had to stop more frequently than they expected, but it was not a big deal because they did not have to arrive at a specific time; it only made the trip seem longer. Lucky rode in her crate in the back of their SUV: Louise set it up so she had her bedtime pillow and one of her chew toys, and she made sure to gave her water every time they stopped. Lucky is usually what Louise calls a chatty dog — she "talks" a lot during the day — but she was almost completely quiet during our two-day drive, so Louise knew she was stressed out.

They did a lot of research before they left to find hotels that accepted pets, and it was a good thing they did because otherwise they would have had a really difficult time finding hotels as they went. Louise thought the only way to do it would have been to stop and ask, and who knows how long that would have taken. They found a fairly common hotel chain that accepts pets, called to confirm that Lucky met their criteria and felt confident that they could stop anywhere along the way as long as they picked one of those hotels. It worked out well for them because they did not want to make reservations in case they felt like driving further or did not want to have to drive so far.

When we finally arrived, it took all of the Callaghans, including Lucky, about six months to feel at home in St. Louis. In Florida, Lucky had a big backyard out in the country, and it took her a while to get used to their much smaller backyard in a busy neighborhood. Their house was smaller, too, and it had two stories where they had been used to a ranch house. But Lucky really loved the dog park near their house, and the girls could not believe that there were some restaurants that let you bring your dog with you to sit outside. Now that they are used to living in St. Louis, it is hard to imagine living anywhere else, and Louise thinks Lucky feels the same way.

# Conclusion

... And They Lived Happily
Ever After

Once you have made a pet part of your family, you and your children will have a lifetime of love and companionship from the animal you have chosen. Of course you will run into some rough patches, but this book should prepare you for many of them so that you can know exactly what you are getting into as pet owners. You will also find that pet ownership brings many rewards for your efforts. Your children will have the pleasure and responsibility of helping to care for a living creature; teaching them how to be good caretakers and giving them an enthusiastic outlet for love and play. Becoming pet owners together is also a wonderful bonding experience for many families, since it gives you an excuse to spend more time together. In fact, if you choose your pet wisely and prepare for it well, adding a pet to your family can be one of the most rewarding tasks your family undertakes together.

Choosing your first pet is a process that cannot and should not be rushed. Take your time and enjoy the opportunity to work through the decision with the rest of your family. Depending on how old your children are, have fun choosing library books with them about different pets or researching pets online together. As you decide what pet is right for you, look for books about your chosen pet so that you can learn more about them and make them part of your bedtime reading. Making your pet selection a thoughtful process and involving the whole family will help your children learn the factors that go into making good decisions and will get them excited about the responsibilities as well as the fun of pet ownership.

A pet is a wonderful addition to your family, and while you should not dwell on those picture-perfect family and pet moments during the process of choosing a pet, you should absolutely enjoy every single one of them after you have brought your pet home.

Congratulations on becoming pet owners and good luck!

# References

Internet

You might find the following Web sites if you need more information on the specific type of pet you and your family has chosen.

American Society for the Prevention of Cruelty to Animals (**www.aspca.org**): This site has lots of information about adopting and caring for pets of all kinds.

Humane Society of the United States (**www.humanesociety.org**): This site is a treasure trove of information, with tips for choosing and finding a pet as well as advice on how to best care for your new pet and current advocacy initiatives.

American Kennel Club (**www.akc.com**): This site operated by the nonprofit American Kennel Club is specifically targeted to the owners of purebred dogs, but owners of mixed breeds can also find some useful information here.

Dogster (**www.dogster.com**): This site has lots of breed-specific information as well as general information on what to expect as a dog owner and how to take care of your pet dog.

Dog Friendly (**www.dogfriendly.com**): Here, you will find first-hand reports about pet friendly accommodations and attractions around the world.

Cat Fanciers (**www.fanciers.com**): This community-oriented site is a wealth of information for cat news, shows, and tips. You will also find a comprehensive list of rescue groups and contact information.

Cat Fanciers' Association (**www.cfainc.org**): This site is targeted toward purebred cats and gives information on cat shows, breeds, and the latest news about the Cat Fanciers' Association.

KittenCare (**www.kittencare.com**): Specifically focused on kittens, this site also contains a lot of information that could be useful for any new cat owner.

Parrot Parrot (**www.parrotparrot.com**): Though it is specifically targeted at parrot owners, this comprehensive site — which includes reviews, tips, and practical information — is a good resource for any bird owner.

United Avian Registry (**www.avianregistry.com**): Owners of all breeds of birds are welcome at this site, where you can register your bird and get information about caring for specific types of birds.

Aquarium Life (**www.aquariumlife.net**): You will find practical fish care advice at this site, plus lots of do-it-yourself projects for your aquarium.

Great Aquarium (**www.greataquarium.com**): This site contains information about choosing fish, setting up your tank and caring for your new pets.

United States Association of Reptile Keepers (**www.usark.org**) This site is packed with information about reptile care and advocacy, as well as common misconceptions about reptiles as pets.

# Bibliography

Kocsis, Anne. *The Complete Guide to Eco-Friendly House Cleaning: Everything You Need to Know Explained Simply.* Atlantic Publishing Group, 2010.

Allred, Alexandra Powe. *Dogs' Most Wanted: The Top 10 Book of Historic Hounds, Professional Pooches, and Canine Oddities.* Potomac Books Inc., 2004.

Alderton, David. *The International Encyclopedia of Pet Care: A Practical Guide to Choosing and Caring for Your Pets.* Howell Books, 1997.

Bricklin, Mark with Gary Burghoff. *Pets as Part of the Family: The Total Care Guide for all the Pets in Your Life (Pets: Part of the Family Books).* Rodale Press, 1999.

Clutton-Brock, Juliet. *Dog.* Dorling Kindersley, 2004.

Crisp, Marty. *Everything Dog: What Kids Really Want to Know About Dogs.* NorthWord Books for Young Readers, 2003.

Holub, Joan. *Why do dogs bark?* New York: Puffin Books, 2001.

Loves, June. *Dogs.* Chelsea Clubhouse, 2004.

Page, Gill. *I Am Your Puppy: An Illustrated Guide to Pet Care for Young Owners.* Waterbird Books, 2004.

Shojai, Amy D. *The First Aid Companion for Dogs & Cats.* Rodale Books, 2001.

Stefoff, Rebecca. *Dogs.* New York: Benchmark Books, 2003.

Fogle, Bruce. *101 Questions Your Cat Would Ask Its Vet: If Your Cat Could Talk.* Tetra Press, 1993.

Head, Honor. *The Artful Kitten.* Courage Books, 1993.

Holland, Barbara. *Secrets of the Cat: Its Lore, Legends, and Lives.* Ivy Books, 1994.

McGinniss, Terry. *The Well Cat Book; The Classic Comprehensive Handbook of Cat Care.* Random House, 1996.

Athan, Mattie Sue. *Guide to a Well-Behaved Parrot.* Barron's Educational Series, 2007.

Gallerstein, Gary A. *The Complete Pet Bird Owner's Handbook.* Avian Publications, 2003.

Higdon, Pam. *Bird Care and Training: An Owner's Guide to a Happy Healthy Pet*. Howell Books, 1998.

Mancini, Julie Rach. *Why Does My Bird Do That: A Guide to Parrot Behavior*. Howell Books, 1998.

Blasiola, George C. and Matthew M. Vriends. *The Saltwater Aquarium Handbook*. Barron's Educational Series, 2000.

Bailey, Mary and Peter Burgess. *Tropical Fishlopaedia: A Complete Guide to Tropical Fish Care*. Howell Books, 2000.

Dawes, John. *Tropical Aquarium Fish: A Step-by-Step Guide to Setting up and Maintaining a Freshwater or Marine Aquarium*. Sterling, 2000.

Sakurai, Atsushi, Yohei Sakamoto and Fumitoshi Mori. *Aquarium Fish of the World: The Comprehensive Guide to 650 Species*. Chronicle Books, 1993.

Wickham, Mike. *What Your Fish Needs*. Dorling Kindersley, 2000.

Alderton, David. *The Exotic Pet Survival Manual: A Comprehensive Guide to Keeping Snakes, Lizards, Other Reptiles, Amphibians, Insects, Arachnids, and Other Invertebrates*. Barron's Educational Series, 1997.

Alderton, David. *A Petkeeper's Guide to Hamsters and Gerbils*. Salamander Press, 1997.

Behrend, Katrin and Karin Skogstad. *The Guinea Pig: How to Care for Them, Feed Them, and Understand Them.* Barron's Educational Series, 1997.

Coborn, John. *The Proper Care of Reptiles.* TFH Publications, 1993.

Frost, Helen. *Hamsters (All About Pets).* New York: Capstone Press, 2001.

Grenard, Steve. *Amphibians: Their Care and Keeping.* Howell Books, 1999.

Gurney, Peter. *The Proper Care of Guinea Pigs.* TFH Publications, 1999.

Hill, Lorraine. *The Really Useful Hamster Guide.* TFH Publications, 1999.

Mattison, Chris. *The Care of Reptiles and Amphibians in Captivity.* Blandford Press, 1992.

Sino, Betsy Sikora. *The Gerbil: An Owner's Guide to a Happy Healthy Pet.* Howell Books, 2000.

# Biography

**Amy Brayfield** is a writer and editor who specializes in parenting, health, and lifestyle topics. She lives in Atlanta with her family, a large yarn stash, and too many books.

# Index

# C

Canaries, 125

Cars, 265

chew toys, 270, 67, 126, 159, 166, 168, 173, 175, 221

Clipping claws, 69

Clipping wings, 117

Cockatiels, 121, 124-125

collar, 106, 163, 37, 245, 264, 67, 93, 228, 230

Collie, 28, 66, 78

Corn snake, 188

Crate training, 74

# D

Declawing, 95

Does, 265, 32, 41, 43, 54, 61, 65, 82, 86, 91, 101, 110, 114, 121, 125, 128, 143, 164, 173-174, 178, 186, 195, 201, 212, 220, 242, 272, 17, 20, 2, 26-27, 29, 32, 35-36, 39-41, 252, 254, 256-257, 261-264, 45, 49, 51, 55, 57, 59, 61, 68, 70, 75, 77, 92, 94, 100-102, 106, 108, 119-121, 134, 155, 161-162, 167-169, 174, 176-177, 187, 195-196, 198, 201-205, 208, 210, 212-213, 220, 228, 234-236, 239, 241, 281, 13, 2

Dog park, 268, 271, 68

# E

end-of-life care, 240

English minks, 160

Exotic pets, 29

# F

filter, 83, 54, 133, 135-136, 146

Flea medication, 67, 93

Fleas, 204, 70, 87, 107, 230, 233

# G

Golden retriever, 62, 18

Goldfish, 38, 47-48, 55, 139, 144

Guppies, 143

# H

Health concerns, 28, 201

Heartworm, 55, 67, 93, 230

Housebreaking, 31, 51, 68, 72-73, 88, 8

Humane Society of the United States, 3, 74, 275, 3

# I

ichthyosporidium, 236

ID, 245, 228

# L

Labrador retriever, 192

Litter Box, 33, 247, 53, 91, 93-94, 96, 98-99, 107-108, 221, 233, 239, 8

Long-hair cat, 100

Lyme disease, 230

# M

Maine Coon, 105

Microchip, 245, 227-228

moving, 68, 107, 224, 30, 243-246, 249, 172

# N

National Association of Professional Pet Sitters, 263

neuter, 37, 54, 67, 93

new baby, 28, 30, 248-251, 258, 47, 146, 220, 223, 10

Nontoxic kitty litter, 98

# O

Obedience-training courses, 194

obsessive grooming, 253

Obstacle course, 268

# P

Parrot, 38, 48, 112, 120, 276, 280

Persian, 103

pet sitter, 261-263

Pet stores, 265, 153, 191, 197, 199, 201-203, 205, 221, 10

Pet-proof, 222

PetCo, 207

Petfinder, 255, 207, 217

PetSmart, 199, 207

Petswelcome.com, 265-266

pH balance, 32

phobias, 252-253

Planes, 263, 46

# R

Rabies, 263

Rainbow fish, 143

re-homing, 254, 217

recurring costs, 38

Rescue groups, 103, 200, 209-216, 223, 276, 10

Russian blues, 160